An Ecopress Book

Ecopress

Dear Phil,
The Shenandoah
is rich in history
and outdoor
recreation
potential.
I
hope you
enjoy this
book.
Sincerely
Bruce Ingram
October 12, 2003

The
Shenandoah
and
Rappahannock
Rivers Guide

By

Bruce Ingram

Ecopress
Corvallis, Oregon

Ecopress

"Books that enhance environmental awareness."

PO Box 2004
Corvallis, OR 97339
Telephone: 1-800-326-9272
Fax: 541-791-2809
Email: ecopress@peak.org
Website: www.ecopress.com
SAN:298-1238

Copyright © 2003

Every effort was made to make this book as accurate and up-to-date as possible. However, there are no warranties expressed or implied, that the information is suitable to any particular purpose. The author and publisher assume no responsibility for activities on the rivers mentioned in this book.

Printed in the U.S. A. on 30% post-consumer recycled paper.

Ingram, Bruce

    The Shenandoah and Rappahannock Rivers Guide / Bruce Ingram

       p. cm.

    ISBN 1-893272-06-0

    1. Outdoor recreation—Virginia—West Virginia—Shenandoah River—Rappahannock River

10 9 8 7 6 5 4 3 2 1

CঙB

To Christian Goebel, who took me on my first trip
   down the South Fork of the Shenandoah;
to Terry Pleskonko, who paddled much of the South
   Fork with me;
to Alec Burnett, who floated most of the Main Stem
   with me;
to Craig Fields, for his passion for the Shenandoah;
to John Garman and Bill Micks for their generous
   help with the Rappahannock, and
to the biologists of the Virginia Department of
   Game and Inland Fisheries and the West Virginia
   Division of Natural Resources, who were a great
   help with this book and with my writing career.

TABLE OF CONTENTS

INTRODUCTION

I love rivers—the moving water, fishing, paddling, birdwatching, wildlife, and history. *The Shenandoah and Rappahannock Rivers Guide* is the third in my guidebook series, following the James and New River guides, and like the other books, this one was a labor of love. As the James and New possess distinctive characteristics, so do the Shenandoah and Rappahannock.

The South Fork and the Main Stem of the Shenandoah are two of the most canoeable rivers in Virginia and West Virginia. Except for a few Class II rapids and where the Main Stem unites with the Potomac near Harpers Ferry, the South Fork and Shenandoah flow very tranquilly. These two rivers are meant for relaxation and enjoying nature in any number of ways. The Rappahannock, in my opinion, is the most beautiful river in the Southeast with its heavily wooded shorelines and lack of human presence. Another commendable trait of the Rap is its lack of access. Once you put in at Kelly's Ford on your voyage to Mott's Run Landing, you have to commit a minimum of two days to the water and the 24½ miles that must be covered. The City of Fredericksburg owns land, which is heavily forested, on both banks of the Rap from Fauquier County downstream to the city limits. And the C.F Phelps Wildlife Management Area (4,539 acres) covers more than five miles of river left shoreline below Kelly's Ford in Fauquier County, another reason for the Rappahannock's isolation. In this day of instant gratification, an excursion down the Rappahannock forces one to drink deeply of the outdoors.

The South Fork of the Shenandoah is born were the South and North Rivers commingle at Port Republic. The Rappahannock comes into existence at Chester Gap in Fauquier County, and the first 60 miles from the headwaters to Mayfield Bridge in Fredericksburg are designated as a State Scenic River. After reading this work, I hope you will designate the South Fork, Main Stem of the Shenandoah, and Rappahannock as three of your favorite waterways.

The Shenandoah and Rappahannock Rivers Guide

Part One
Making the Most of Your Day on the Water

What better way for a couple to spend time together than canoeing and/ or fishing a river. Here Angela and Christian Goebel do just that.

1.1
RIVERS AND ROMANCE IN VIRGINIA

One of the best ways my wife Elaine and I spend quality time together is canoeing Virginia's four major highland rivers: the James, New, Rappahannock, and South Fork of the Shenandoah. We aren't interested in running Class III rapids that require deft maneuvers and advanced paddling skills. But we do relish those excursions where we can drift lazily along, observe wildlife, fish, and most importantly revel together in the beauty of the surrounding mountains and rural countryside.

And when our day on the water concludes, the two of us often head for a nearby restaurant and a local bed and breakfast. Here, then, is a couple-friendly float trip from each of the streams, and great places for romance and relaxation afterwards.

James River

A beautiful outing on the upper James is the seven-miler from Alpine to Natural Bridge Station in Botetourt and Rockbridge counties. The river left put-in is across from an abandoned store on Route 608/622.

Our favorite part of this excursion is some remains of the James River and Kanawha Canal that tower above the stream on river left about two miles into the float. The canal, with George Washington as a major supporter and with a grandiose goal of connecting its two name-sake rivers, served as a major conduit for commerce until the mid 1800s. But the coming of the railroads and the Civil War doomed this ambitious project. We like to take Kodachromes of the rock structure and partake of a shore lunch on a small island directly across from the canal remains.

This trek also teems with wildlife. The Jefferson National Forest borders the James on river right for much of the trip and forest birds such as wood thrushes, Carolina wrens, and ovenbirds frequently add their voices to the surroundings.

Another scenic section occurs about five miles from the put-in. An easy Class I rapid, formed by a three-foot high ledge, punctuates the river and forms a rock-studded pool. Look upstream from the pool and you'll espy an enchanting combination of mountains, forested shoreline, and rapids.

The river left take-out at Natural Bridge Station (located on Route 759 next to a lumberyard) exists several hundred yards below an ebony railroad bridge, which looks as if it has sunk in the middle. In reality, this is an optical illusion, but the pleasures found on this trip definitely are not.

The Rappahannock

Although we live close to and enjoy the James and New, I must admit that the Rappahannock is the most beautiful river Elaine and I have ever canoed. It is not mere chance, however, that this river, located in the heavily populated Northern Virginia area, continues to flow through a pristine setting.

Much of the Rappahannock is protected under the Scenic River

Act, and many enlightened landowners have tried to maintain the sylvan setting of the watershed. Also in many places, the city of Fredericksburg owns the banks on both sides of the Rap and the city planners have recognized that the river is the crown jewel of Old Dominion waterways.

The only drawback for some paddlers is that they must commit to a two-day float. The premier section is the 24½ miles from Kelly's Ford on Route 620 to Motts Run Landing (both access points on river right) in Fredericksburg, a trek too far to cover in a day.

The best way to tackle this section is to canoe 16 miles the first day to the confluence of the Rappahannock and Rapidan rivers. A number of campsites dot the river right shoreline, especially at the confluence and the first several hundred yards below it. Then you can leisurely make your way to Mott's Landing the following day, and recuperate at the many restaurants and B&Bs in Fredericksburg and Spotsylvania County.

Two scenic areas stand out on the first leg of the journey. An inviting place is Snake Castle Rock, a cabin-sized boulder that occurs on river left several hours into the junket. A small island of aquatic grass, a deep pool, and a sandy bank make this area a charming place to swim, bask in the sun, and dine on a shore lunch.

The other is an outside bend that occurs just above the confluence. Expect to see ospreys, belted kingfishers, and perhaps even a bald eagle along this river left curve in the Rap. Sycamores, silver maples, and river birch form a dense canopy along the shoreline. Most importantly, the Rappahannock itself proves that an idyllic river can survive the environmental destruction of the twentieth century, and today serve as a refuge for wildlife and for those who love rivers.

South Fork of the Shenandoah

Many years ago, I took my first junket down the South Fork of the Shenandoah, the Bixlers Bridge to Foster's trip, and today this nine-miler remains a favorite. Christian Goebel of Shenandoah River Outfitters in Luray relates that this outing is ideal for novice paddlers because of its gentle flow and gorgeous surroundings.

Perhaps the prettiest section occurs on the last mile of the float.

There the Blue Ridge Mountains dominate the horizon ahead and the Massanutten Mountains command the view behind. Several riffles speckle the river through this area, one of which features a nearby Indian fish trap.

Native Americans built these upside down V rock formations from bank to bank and just under the surface. To alarm fish, these resourceful people dragged stones attached to grapevines along the bottom and herded the fish into the enclosure where they were netted. Interestingly, the word "Shenandoah" is Native American for "Daughter of the Stars," an appropriate appellation for such a heavenly waterway.

Another marvelous section comes into view about half way into the excursion. A series of farms, meadows, and weathered barns combine with the Massanutten Mountains to create a visually stunning backdrop. Overall, the South Fork of the Shenandoah probably offers more easy-to-negotiate float trips than any other major river in the Old Dominion.

The New River

The New is known for its whitewater, but actually hosts several tranquil sections. One of those is the 12-miler from Independence to Baywood, which is a very pleasant float through rural countryside and one that is perfect for beginners. The river left put-in is located on Route 700, off Route 21. The river right take-out lies just past the Route 58/221 Bridge.

One of the most picturesque sections occurs about half way through when the mountains can be seen from both sides of the upper New. Quite a few older homesteads dot both shorelines, and a nice mixture of woodlots, fields, and barns lie near the river. Because of this habitat's diversity, a wide variety of songbirds nest along this section. Expect to hear forest birds such as hooded warblers, red-eyed vireos, and tufted titmice one moment and edge or field avians such as white-eyed vireos, meadowlarks, and field sparrows a short time later.

Another favorite spot is where the Little River enters the New on river right. Just downstream from the confluence rests a sandy beach that is a popular place to take a break and to compose pictures of the surrounding mountains.

Canoeing Virginia's four most popular highland rivers is a joyous way to pass time with a spouse. It's just as good, in fact, as spending romantic moments that evening at a restaurant, followed by a night at a bed and breakfast!

Trip Planner

Anyone, regardless of his or her canoeing skills, should contact an outfitter before planning that maiden trip down any river. And before a float, I like to call liveries to find out current stream and weather conditions. Liveries are quite willing to tutor novices by explaining basic strokes and how to avoid difficult situations. Tourism agencies can supply valuable trip planning information as well, including information about restaurants and accommodations. Following are information sources for each of the rivers mentioned in this chapter.

A. JAMES

Lodging

Lynchburg is home for several of the B&Bs listed below, and the James flows through this city. The Natural Bridge Station take-out is less than an hour away. The Lynchburg area offers several couple-friendly trips such as Six-Mile Bridge to Joshua Falls (4 miles) and Joshua Falls to Galt's Mill (3½ miles).
Dulwich Manor (800-571-9011) in Amherst
Federal Crest Inn (800-818-6155) in Lynchburg
Winridge (804-384-7220) in Madison Heights

Recommended Restaurants
(all except Natural Bridge Hotel located in Lynchburg)
Crown Sterling (804-239-7744)
Merriwethers (804-384-3311)
Natural Bridge Hotel (800-533-1410)
Poplar Grille at Holiday Inn Select (804-528-2500)
Sachiko's International Restaurant (804-237-5655)
Trotters (804-846-3545)

Outfitters
James River Paddle Sports (804-384-3636) in Monroe

Tourism Info
Lynchburg Visitors Information Center (800-732-5821)

B. RAPPAHANNOCK

Lodging
La Vista Plantation (800-529-2823) in Fredericksburg
Littlepage Inn (800-248-1803) in Spotsylvania County
On Keegan Pond B&B (888-785-4662) in Spotsylvania County
Roxbury Mill B&B (540-582-6611) in Spotsylvania County
The Guest House at Walnut Grove (540-854-7773) in Spotsylvania
   County

Recommended Restaurant
Olde Mudd Tavern (540-582-5250) in Spotsylvania County.

Outfitters
(all in Fredericksburg)
   Clore Brothers Outfitters (800-704-7749)
   Virginia Outdoor Center (877-PLAY-VA2)
   Rappahannock River Campground (800-784-7235).
Tourism Info
Fredericksburg Area Tourism (800-654-4118)
Fredericksburg Visitor Center (800-678-4748)

C. SOUTH FORK OF THE SHENANDOAH

Lodging
(all except Milton House located in Front Royal)
   Chester House (800—621-0441)
   Milton House B&B Inn (800-816-3731) in Stanley
   Tanglewood B&B (888-300-9257
   Woodward House (800-635-7011)

Recommended Restaurants
(all in Front Royal)
  J's Gourmet (540-636-9293)
  14th Street Bistro (540-636-8408)

Outfitters
  Front Royal Canoe Company (800-270-8808)
  Shenandoah River Trips (800-RAPIDS1) in Bentonville
  Shenandoah River Outfitters (800-6CANOE2) in Luray

Tourism Info
  Front Royal/Warren County Visitors Center (800-338-2576)

D. NEW

Lodging
  Fox Hill Inn (800-874-3313) in Troutdale

Recommended Restaurants
  Mountain House Restaurant (336-359-2580) in Piney Creek, NC
  Shatley Springs Inn (336-982-2236) in Crumpler, NC
Outfitter
  New River Canoe & Campground (276-773-3412) in Independence

Tourism Info
  Grayson County Tourism Information Center (276-773-3711)

E. MAPS

  Virginia Department of Game & Inland Fisheries (804-367-1000)
  Virginia Atlas & Gazetteer (800-452-5931)
  Maptech (800-627-7236), topo maps on CD ROM

Choosing the right lures can make a difference when fishing rivers.

1.2
A PRIMER ON FISHING SMALLMOUTH RIVERS

Over the past five years or so, I have noticed that the small-mouth rivers where I regularly fish in Virginia and West Virginia have been receiving a great deal more interest and fishing pressure from the angling public. As much as I enjoy lake fishing for largemouth bass, I understand this surge in popularity, as my real passion is river small-mouth angling. If I have the option of drifting down a scenic river and catching several smallmouths between 12 and 18 inches every hour, or competing with a half dozen other anglers to work a dock while jet boaters and water skiers careen by, little doubt exists which choice I will make. If you are new to river fishing or are a veteran river runner who wants to catch better quality bronzebacks, this primer is for you.

How to Read Moving Water

Every aspect of river smallmouth fishing begins with knowing how to read moving water. And the focal points of that knowledge are the Class I, II, and III rapids that punctuate the nation's premier small-mouth rivers. Rapids dictate how and where the bass will hold both above and well below these drops in the stream bottom.

For example, approximately 50 to 100 yards above every rapid, "push water" begins. This is a section where the current begins to pick up more speed as the declination in the stream comes nearer. One of the surer things about bass fishing is that push water holds active smallies. The food chain is in motion here as hordes of predators attempt to consume myriad prey.

Many anglers new to river smallmouth fishing may be surprised to learn that the spot where the stream bottom actually declines, the rapid itself, is often a very poor place to catch quality fish. Larger mossybacks are simply not going to battle the heavy current there. Instead, concentrate your efforts on two kinds of current breaks below the rapid itself.

Perhaps the best form of current break is an eddy. Eddies, which are places where the current reverses upon itself, typically form in "walls" to the right or left of the main flow. By their nature, eddies (some anglers call them whirlpools) tend to trap minnows, crayfish, sculpins, hellgrammites, and other creatures within their boundaries. Smallmouths seem to instinctively know this, making eddies yet another place where actively foraging fish will gather.

The second major kind of current break found directly below a rapid is a large rock or boulder. Smallmouths find respite from the current here, holding directly behind these sanctuaries only to dash out when hapless prey species pass close by. Current breaks are obviously easy to spot when the upper sections of rocks rise above the surface. But subsurface rocks are almost as easy to find if you will make note of "boils," that is, little pockets of water that appear to have "churned up and over" the surrounding liquid. Work boils hard, as many anglers overlook them.

Which Structure and Cover Forms Hold the Best Fish

Once you have left a rapid and the eddies and current breaks that form immediately below, the next step is to locate the various forms of structure and cover that typically exist until the next rapid looms. By

14

far, my favorite form of river structure is a deep-water ledge. Ledges, sometimes known as shoals, often run across a river, but they can parallel the flow as well. No matter, either type of ledge is an excellent foraging ground for smallmouths.

The dark sanctums of a ledge (and the best ones often lie five or more feet beneath the surface with only their tips above the water line) are natural feeding and hiding grounds for crayfish. It's not surprising that the vast majority of the 4-pound smallmouths (the benchmark for a trophy river smallie just about anywhere in the country) that I have caught have come from ledges. Spend plenty of time probing these lairs.

A second form of structure is a rocky dropoff along the main channel. Often the only sign of a below surface dropoff is that the river will seem to pick up speed for a brief period of time. Much harder to

The "Universal" Worm

I have probably caught more quality river smallmouths on 6-inch Mister Twister Phenoms in pumpkinpepper or black than on any other baits. Chuck Byrd, general manager for Mister Twister, maintains that there is no mystery why curly-tailed annelids are so effective.

"The simple answer is that a curly-tailed worm will produce on lakes, reservoirs, rivers, and ponds anywhere in the country," he says. "On rivers, the right colored worm, retrieved in the right way, can be made to look like a nightcrawler, hellgrammite, minnow, or just about anything else."

"After the worm, I would rate the grub as the next best universal bait, especially on rivers. A 3- or 4-inch grub can be retrieved to look like a crawfish, minnow, shad, or a leech. Just change colors and retrieves to create the effect you want."

find and work than ledges, dropoffs possess big bass potential. To work a dropoff, position your boat at a sharp angle to the declination and point the bow upstream. You will be able to execute several casts before the current carries you downstream.

The farther you float from a rapid, the more important bank cover becomes. Like lake anglers, I like to check out submerged logs that lie in four or more feet of water along a river bank. If these logs rest within indentations or cuts in the shoreline, so much the better.

Another superlative form of wood cover is a root system created by shoreline dwelling trees. Typically known as "wads," these roots create marvelous ambush points for oversize mossybacks. Across much of smallmouth country, sycamore trees engender the most cherished root wads. Other quality forms of wood cover include brush piles, stickups, and the various pieces of flotsam that come to rest in outside bends.

Which Lures to Select

If you are a lake angler who wants to become better at river fishing, you won't need an entire new selection of baits or rods. Indeed, I employ basically the same lineup of lures and outfits that I do for impoundment bassing.

For example, from mid-to-late spring through early-to-mid fall, I rely on the same quartet of rods. On a six-foot medium action spinning rod, I typically have a ¼-ounce buzzbait affixed. I have such faith in buzzbaits that I will throw them all day throughout the warm water period. A second and similar outfit is what I call my "variable" topwater rod. Depending on the whims of the fish and myself, I will rotate among Heddon Tiny Torpedoes, Rebel Pop'Rs, Storm Chug Bugs, Rapala Skitter Pops and Props, and Phillips Crippled Killers among others. Even if several of these artificials are not producing, chances are that one of them will. Both of these outfits are coupled with 8- or 10-pound test Trilene XL.

The third rod is a medium heavy 6½ -foot baitcaster spooled with 12-pound test line. This is my favorite outfit for probing deep-water ledges, and I will opt for a 1/4 to 3/8-ounce jig and soft plastic trailer or a 6-inch Texas rigged plastic worm tied to the business end of the line. The fourth outfit is a medium heavy 6½-foot spinning rod, and it comes with 10-pound test. (If the water is extremely clear, this outfit will receive greater use than the baitcaster.) I typically rotate among 4-inch grubs, craw worms, ringworms, and plastic lizards for this rod.

Occasionally, especially in the pre-spawn period, I will bring along a fifth rod, this one a medium action, 6½-foot spinning outfit, that I use for crankbaits. But for most of the warm water period, the above four outfits will suffice quite well.

Seasonal Tips for Overgrown River Smallmouths

Again like their lake largemouth counterparts, river smallmouth enthusiasts are becoming more four-season anglers. Following are my favorite patterns for the major periods of the year.

Tubes:
The Current Hot Bait for Current Dwelling Bass

Two of my hottest baits for big smallmouths was the 3½-inch Venom tube and Strike King, Kevin VanDam Pro-Model Tube. Chris Armstrong, public relations manager for Strike King, relates that river fishermen have noted the success that lake anglers have had recently with tubes and have made these lures their go-to baits as well.

"In the past, the only time you would see a river angler use a tube is when a cold front existed," says Armstrong. "And, then, that individual would rely on those 2-inch or so finesse tubes that were so popular."

"Today, river anglers are using the same large tubes that lake anglers are. And both groups often fish them the same way: that is, Texas-rigged with a sliding bullet sinker and with the bait retrieved slowly across the bottom. Regardless of whether you are on a lake or a river, a tube resting on the bottom with its tentacles waving about says crawfish. And that kind of motion will attract bass anywhere."

To target bruiser bronzebacks during the cold water period, camp out on deep-water ledges well away from heavy current. Dredge the bottom with a jig and soft plastic trailer combo and inch the bait along. Expect only four or five bites per day and be mentally prepared that you will only connect on two or three of those strikes. But the few fish you have on will be dandies.

During the pre-spawn period, crank laydowns and brush piles along the shoreline. For best results, retrieve your crankbaits in a variety of speeds, but always try to make them bounce off wood. Evening sport tends to be much better than morning action.

For post-spawn smallies, swim three or 4-inch grubs or "lift-pause-lift" 6-inch plastic worms around current breaks such as boulders. River smallmouths tend to feed much more aggressively after the spawn than do lake bass of any species.

The summer months are my favorite period to be on America's rivers. This is topwater time at its best; and unlike lake largemouths, stream bronzebacks will clobber topwaters all day long, even during the dog days. Eddies are where the action is often best; but anywhere shade exists, you are likely to contact fish.

Fall is the season when anything goes on rivers. Every one of the aforementioned patterns may be in play or only one of them will. Be prepared to tie on any of the lures in your tacklebox and to check out every form of cover, structure, or current break. Also realize that no pattern seems to last more than a few hours on any given day.

For those of us like myself whose primary piscatorial passion is chasing after river smallmouths, no other kind of angling can compete in terms of providing pleasure. I hope this primer will serve to make you interested in visiting the waterway nearest you or has given you insight on how to make your time more productive on your home river.

Understanding how the weather affects birds can lead to fishing success.

1.3
LET BIRDS BE FISH AND GAME INDICATORS

Before an excursion down the James River one June, I did what I always do, check the Weather Channel for the latest forecast. The weather had been noticeably cooler the previous three days, and I had hoped that the series of summer cold fronts moving through the area had departed.

The morning forecast was not promising, however. The weather summary noted that the wind was from the northeast, a sure sign of a cold front, and the daytime high was not expected to top seventy degrees. Nevertheless, I felt that I could cope with the conditions, until I arrived at the boat ramp and saw a row of bank swallows sitting on a telephone wire.

"This is not good," I said, pointing up at the swallows as a friend and I began our trip. "Those swallows should be out chasing insects by now. I think the whole food chain has shut down and that the fishing will be poor this morning."

19

My buddy looked at me as if I had lost my mind. What, he questioned, do birds have to do whether or not the fishing will be good? Four hours later, after we had combined to catch just two decent bass and we had witnessed very few fish of any kind feeding, my canoeing companion was ready to admit that just maybe those bank swallows had been on to something. I strongly believe that birds of various kinds are not only indicators of fishing success, but that their presence, or absence, can also tell a sportsman a great deal about whether or not he will be successful in Virginia's forests.

Birds as Fishing Indicators

Several kinds of birds are marvelous indicators of whether or not such species as smallmouth and largemouth bass will be in an area. For example, smallmouth bass and avians such as great blue herons, green herons, and belted kingfishers share several common traits: they are all predators and they all consume minnows.

Water willow beds thrive along many rivers, often growing adjacent to shallow, rocky bottoms. Whenever I view great blue or green herons stalking the edges of water willow or espy a belted kingfisher perched on a snag above this aquatic grass, I know that the "fishing" will likely be good for both the birds and me. Smallmouth bass are attracted to the minnows near the water willow just as the birds are.

On lakes, I regard the presence of ospreys as a very positive sign. For instance, ospreys prefer soft-rayed fish such as those in the minnow and shad families. Spot an osprey plunging feet first into an area numerous times over the course of a morning, and you'll likely find largemouth bass feeding on those same baitfish.

On trout streams, I associate several species of warblers with superb fishing. Louisiana waterthrush are a prime example of this. This species prefers shaded areas along brooks and ravines, especially if the water in those locales flows briskly along. If I am hiking along a trout stream and hear the musical whistles of the Louisiana up ahead, I become hopeful that some brookies also share the same area.

Hooded warblers are another songbird that thrives along upland rills. This warbler frequents heavily wooded areas, mountain laurel, and shady stream banks, exactly the kind of habitat that often offers prime trout angling. Hearken to the sound of the hooded's "tooe, tooe, tee-to" and limber up the long rod.

Birds as Hunting Indicators

If hunters could learn to recognize the appearance and song of just one species of bird, I would recommend the Carolina wren. This sparrow-sized songbird (reddish brown above and buff below) is definitely the "busybody, the nosy neighbor" among the creatures that inhabit woodlands.

Many times I have been on stand and heard the "buzzy" sound of the Carolina's alarm note (sort of a "chirrrr"). Get ready! A deer, turkey, squirrel, or even a bear may be on the way. This wren feels compelled to sound off when other creatures enter its territory. Another game indicator is a blue jay. For instance, one early autumn morning I was scouting a woodlot where I often pursue squirrels and bowhunt for deer. I heard a series of the trumpeting whistles and twitters that blue jays utter up ahead. Arriving at the source of the racket (blue jays are no wood thrushes when it comes to making melody), I espied a flock of jays flitting about in a massive scarlet oak.

This member of the red oak family was dripping acorns, whereas most of the other oaks in the area had produced very poor mast crops. That autumn the hunting for the squirrels and whitetails in the area was phenomenal. The game animals, along with the jays, were all gorging on the scarlet oak acorns.

Spring gobbler enthusiasts would do well to learn the "cuk-cuk-cukcuk" of the pileated woodpecker. The East's largest woodpecker, roughly the size of a crow, possesses a red crest and flashes white under wings in flight. I first learned the importance of recognizing the vocalizations of the pileated many years ago while turkey hunting. The morning had been lacking in gobbling when I heard the notes of the pileated. I listened closer and detected the faint sounds of a hen clucking every time the pileated sounded off, or was the pileated responding to the hen? In any event, I quickly made a loud cutting sound with a mouth call, and a gobbler issued his response.

Interestingly, over the past few years, turkey call manufacturers have begun to make pileated woodpecker calls, advertising them as great offbeat locator calls for gobblers, which they are. If your usual yelps, clucks, and purrs are not engendering a response, try the pileated woodpecker call to ascertain if there are any hens or toms in the vicinity.

Another way that songbirds can be game indicators is that prime songbird habitat can often be superlative game habitat, and vice-versa. For instance, I own some acreage where I have let the fencerows become quite overgrown on purpose. Those fencerows harbor excellent numbers of rufous-sided towhees, song sparrows, white-eyed vireos, and often a covey of bobwhite quail and some rabbits. Several acquaintances have admonished me to tidy up the place for "the sake of appearances," but the bobs, bunnies and songbirds seem to like matters just fine.

Summing Up

Remember that fruitless fishing morning mentioned earlier in this story? Later that day in the afternoon, the wind shifted to being from the southwest, and my friend and I noticed bank swallows dipping about close to the James' surface up ahead. Paddling closer, we saw a damselfly hatch taking place and the bronzebacks slashing about on the surface to take advantage of it. At a water willow bed to our right, two great blue herons were stalking the grass line. And on a sycamore-shrouded shoreline to our left, we heard an orchard oriole singing nonstop. The smallmouth sport was superlative the rest of the afternoon. Indeed, birds can be outstanding indicators of whether fishing or hunting can be rewarding.

Roger Stultz of Roanoke with a North Fork of the Shenandoah trout.

1.4
A TRIBUTE TO TRIBUTARIES:
TROUT FISHING IN THE SHENANDOAH SYSTEM

Around the year 1400 A.D., poet Geoffrey Chaucer wrote, and I paraphrase, that when the sweet showers of April come, then folks long to go on pilgrimages. Today, when the spring rains swell the streams that flow into the North and South Forks of the Shenandoah, many fishing folk long to make pilgrimages to those tributaries that course through glen and dell.

Early one April, my son Mark an I took our own April journey from Botetourt County to join Owen Stultz and his son Roger, both of Roanoke, for a sojourn in Rockingham County. Our "Canterbury" was the headwaters of the North Fork of the Shenandoah and one of its nearby tributaries, the German River.

At the German River near the community of Bergton, both Mark and I landed brook trout, their vibrant colors indicating that they had plenty of time to adapt to stream life. My fifteen-year-old son was especially pleased to have won his first battle with a brookie. Mark said the trout was too beautiful to keep and released the fish back into the German.

Later, the four of us traveled a short distance to the headwaters of the North Fork of the Shenandoah, which the German River flows into. Browns were the most often caught salmonid there as my group tangled with several nice, stocked fish. The day was made complete when Owen's wife Flemmie served baked brown trout for dinner.

This chapter will feature a number of the trout streams (and descriptions of them) that flow into the North and South Forks of the Shenandoah. You and yours may want to go on pilgrimages to some of these tributaries this spring.

Native Trout Streams and the German River

Named for the hardy German settlers that migrated from Pennsylvania and Maryland to establish homesteads in the Shenandoah Valley, the German River today is stocked once in November and in December, and once in April and in May. Roger Stultz, a supervisor for Roanoke City Social Services, says the stream has long been a part of his family history.

"From back in the 1700s and 1800s, so much of my family has lived near the German River in the Bergton area that I feel a real attachment to the stream," says Stultz. "Some of my family even lived back in the mountains near the native brook trout streams that flow into the German. One of my earliest members was from almost 40 years ago when my dad, who is now 74, took me back into the mountains."

"We climbed to a mountain peak and then followed a little trickle of water down until it turned into a brook trout stream. I was with my dad for a week fishing, and we only saw one other person the entire time. Dad even showed me the enclosures where the state held deer until they could be acclimated to their surroundings and released. Those enclosures were from a time years before when there were few deer in the mountains. Today, you can still go up into the mountains and fish these secluded native trout streams."

Roger Stultz describes the German River as being a beautiful stream, replete with rhododendron, riffles, and heavily wooded banks.

German River Road parallels the waterway for much of its path through Rockingham County, but while wading the stream, one often gets the impression that civilization is far away.

"I hope people will always cherish trout streams like the German River," says Stultz. "Future generations should have the German to enjoy. I hope society will see the benefits of taking care of this stream and its watershed and protecting them from poultry farm run-off and other forms of pollution."

North Fork of the Shenandoah

Many sportsmen don't realize that the North Fork of the Shenandoah is much more than a quality smallmouth river. At its headwaters in Rockingham County, the North Fork is a fine trout stream and is stocked once in November and December and in January and February, once in March, and twice between early April and May 15. Owen Stultz, a retired minister, has fished the river for some 70 years.

"I think that the upper North Fork is a superb stocked trout stream that flows through a very scenic area," he says. "The most beautiful sight, I think, near the North Fork is Chimney Rock. It is a huge, natural rock that has a top with a curve to it."

"Typically, the river passes by agricultural areas and wooded shorelines. The best trout fishing takes place above the Fulks Run area. Below there in the Cootes Store area, smallmouth bass and redeyes are the most common fish."

Stultz relates that Route 259 in Rockingham County parallels or comes near much of the upper North Fork. Thus, access is quite good, and the river often receives considerable fishing pressure on weekends and after stockings have taken place. Visitors may want to do what my son and I did, that is fish the German River in the morning and ply the North Fork in the afternoon.

Passage Creek

Passage Creek in Warren County flows into the North Fork of the Shenandoah near Front Royal. This stream is part of Virginia's delayed harvest program in which catchable size trout are stocked in the fall, winter, and spring. From October 1 through May 31 each year, anglers may employ only single hook artificial lures, and trout must be immediately released. From June 1 through September 30, general trout regulations are in effect. Anglers must possess a trout license to fish delayed harvest streams from October 1 through June 15.

On Passage Creek, the delayed harvest section extends from the Warren County line downstream for one mile through the Front Royal Fish Hatchery. Tom Sadler operates Two Dogs Trading Company, a guide service in Fauquier County.

"Passage Creek is a freestone stream that is a good place for novice flyfishermen or people just starting to spin fish for trout to go," he says. "The creek is heavily stocked, but the downside is that Passage does receive a lot of pressure because the access is very good. The stream is fairly open, so a beginner doesn't have to worry about snagging in the trees so much."

"I would also describe Passage as a valley-type stream. The banks are not very steep, the gradient is average, and some deep pools exist. Something I really like about Passage Creek is that the scenery surrounding it is quite beautiful and wide open like you would see out West. This stream is one where I would take a family to fish."

Sadler confesses that his favorite time to visit Passage Creek is during January when the stream is typically deserted.

Jeremys Run

Jeremys Run courses through the Shenandoah National Park (SNP) on its way to unite with the South Fork near Rileyville. Sadler describes it as a classic, SNP freestone mountain stream.

"If you hike in to fish Jeremys Run, be prepared to work up a sweat," he says. "To reach the creek, you have to go in from the top of the Skyline Drive and take a steep hike down into a mountain valley. The hike down is bad enough, but the hike out is much more difficult. The whole experience can be an ordeal, but the fishing is worth the effort."

"Jeremys Run has numerous plunge pools with a lot of pocket water. The water is often so clear that you can do some sight-fishing. A hiking trail also runs beside the creek. All kinds of wildlife from black bear to songbirds live along the stream."

Sadler adds that because Jeremys is so narrow in width, anglers might want to opt for 7½-foot flyrods. Brook trout between five and nine inches fin the waters there.

Stony Creek

One of the most popular stocked trout streams in Virginia is Stony Creek in the Edinburg area. This tributary of the North Fork typically receives monthly infusions of trout between October and May.

In the spring, Class I and II rapids punctuate this stream, and the occasional Class III can metamorphose if water levels are high. At its headwaters, Stony tumbles through the mountains of the George Washington National Forest. Near its confluence, the creek runs through Edinburg. In between, Stony flows through farmlands, fields, and forests.

A major tributary is Little Stony Creek; a special regulation wild trout stream. On the portion located within the national forest, anglers can only use single hook, artificial lures and all trout less than nine inches must be released. Adult brookies average in the seven to nine inch size range.

South River

The South River's mouth, near Port Republic, unites with the North River to begin the South Fork of the Shenandoah. There the South River features smallmouth bass and redeye angling. The gradient is quite gentle for the most part.

Well upstream, the South offers a delayed harvest section in Waynesboro from the base of Rife Loth Dam to 2.4 miles downstream to the Second Street Bridge. This is urban trout fishing at its finest as the stream sports plenty of trout and numerous runs and riffles. In the Grottoes area, the South River reverts to regular trout fishing regulations and typically receives monthly stockings October through February and twice per month in the spring.

The South River sports some important tributaries, including Paine Run which flows through the Shenandoah National Park. Also, Back Creek and Mills Creek are a part of the drainage far upstream on the South River.

South Fork Tributaries

The South Fork of the Shenandoah is strictly a warm-water stream, but several of its tributaries conceal native trout, especially those that wind their ways through the Shenandoah National Park. A few wild trout streams include Madison Run, Big Run, and Naked Creek. Hawksbill Creek is a popular stocked trout stream that enters the South Fork near Alma.

SNP streams come under several special regulations. For instance, most streams open to angling require catch and release. And all fishing is restricted to the use of single hook artificial lures. Where harvest is allowed, trout must be nine inches or more in length, and the creel limit is six trout per day. Anglers are nevertheless encouraged to release all native brook trout.

Alec Burnett, owner and chief guide for Shenandoah Lodge and Outfitters in Luray, proclaims Madison Run as being a fine stream in the spring, specifically if a good snow pack occurred during the winter. The guide describes Madison as being a "tight creek to fish" with its narrow channel and vegetation covered shorelines. Stealth is a must, Burnett emphasizes, and he often lies prone while dropping a fly into Madison. Burnett also describes Madison as being one of the more heavily fished streams in the SNP. The stream is fairly easy to access, which is the major cause for the fishing pressure.

Page County's Hawksbill Creek generally receives stockings once a month November through March and twice between the first of April and May 15. At one time, Hawksbill Creek suffered from water quality problems and stockings ceased; those problems have now been corrected.

"Hawksbill Creek flows well up in the SNP, though the stream is smaller than the Rapidan River," says Burnett. "Down in the valley, the best place to fish is from the Route 211/340 intersection upstream for about three miles through the town of Luray. The access is good, and I have seen rainbows, up to 20 inches, finning pools in downtown Luray."

How-to Tips

For spring action, Tom Sadler recommends size 16-20 Blue-Wing Olives and black or green size 12-14 streamers. These are all general patterns if any dark fly hatch is taking place. If the flies coming off are light-colored, continues the guide, prudent choices are Yellow Sallies or any sulfur imitation in size 16-20. Also productive are Pheasant Tale Nymphs and Harry Murray's Mr. Rapidan, both in size 16-18.

Sadler prefers medium fast action 6½-foot rods in 2- or 3-weight; his favorite is the Thornton River Special, made by Paul Kearny of the Thornton River Fly Shop. Shorter rods are ideal for working in the often cramped confines of many Shenandoah Valley streams, especially those in the SNP. Sadler pairs these rods with a nine-foot leader tapered down to 6x and an 18 to 24-inch tippet in 6x. Avoid letting your leader become much less than 18 inches long he admonishes.

Guide Alec Burnett maintains that summer brings forth its own unique kind of challenges.

"You can be on a Shenandoah Valley stream at mid-morning and, let's say hypothetically, that a tan caddis-type hatch comes off," he says. "You try to match that hatch, and you can't get a strike."

"The solution for that problem, and many other match the hatch type problems that appear, is to tie on a size 14 to 24 dry Adams, depending on the size of the fly that is hatching and the size of the water. For example, I go with smaller size flies in the SNP, but larger ones on the stocked trout streams. Why the Adams always seems to work is a mystery to me, but this pattern has been successful for probably a hundred years or more."

"A marvelous backup fly," continues Burnett, "is a parachute Adams in that same size range. Parachutes sit lower in the water and a bit of orange, white, or red indicator will enable a long rodder to better determine if the fly has attracted attention in the form of a sipping salmonid."

Burnett also favors size 12-14 Black Ants and size 20-24 Griffith Gnats. His choice for a summer rod is a 6½- to 7½-foot model in the 2- to 4-weight range. The guide pairs this outfit with a 12- to 15-foot double tapered leader (either 5x or 6x) and a 12- to 16-inch tippet of 5x or 6x.

The Shenandoah Valley is famous for many things: Civil War battles, pastoral farms, the majestic Blue Ridge and Massanutten mountain chains, and some of the best trout fishing in the Southeast. Indeed, the trout streams that feed into the North and South Forks are so numerous that I can't possibly cover them all here or adequately cover the ones that I did mention. Having too many quality trout streams to cover, or to fish, is not a bad problem to have, especially if you yearn for a fishing pilgrimage.

IF YOU GO

For guided trips with Tom Sadler, contact him at Two Dogs Trading Company (540-253-7430) or tom@twodogstradingco.com. For guided trips with Alec Burnett, contact him at Shenandoah Lodge and Outfitters at (800) 866-9958 or flyfish@shentel.net. For more information on the SNP (Shenandoah National Park), dial (540) 999-3500. Another information source is the Virginia Department of Game and Inland Fisheries office at Verona: (540) 248-9360. A good source for information and productive patterns is the Thornton River Fly Shop at (540) 987-9400.

Caledonia Farm-1812 B&B is under a conservation easement.

1.5
HOW ONE LANDOWNER PROTECTED HIS LAND FOR POSTERITY,
AND HOW YOU CAN, TOO

Caledonia Farm—1812 B&B in Flint Hill, Virginia, looks today much as it did when first built nearly two hundred years ago. The stone manor house is the second dwelling to have been constructed on the two thousand-acre original Lord Fairfax grant. And thanks to Phil Irwin's foresight, 85 of those acres, along with the home and three-fourths mile of stone fencing remain intact today.

In 1974, Irwin became the first landowner in Rappahannock County, Virginia to bestow an easement to the Virginia Outdoors Foundation (VOF) when he did so with his B&B. In 2000, Irwin created additional protection for the property when he donated an easement on agricultural land directly across the rural road from Caledonia, ensuring that the pastoral setting of the farm would also be preserved.

Caledonia Farm is no ordinary B&B, making Irwin's easement of no small consequence. The property lies at the base of "The Peak," a majestic mountain in the Shenandoah National Park. The working farm is also within sight of the Skyline National Scenic Drive. Agricultural lands, orchards, pastures, stone and chestnut fencing, forested areas, and mountain views characterize the general area. And the acres of Caledonia Farm house the headwaters of streams that are part of the Rappahannock River watershed.

Additionally, Caledonia Farm is on both the Virginia Landmarks Register and the National Register of Historic Places. Caledonia Farm is the only B&B in the area with such distinctions. These designations mean that, in spite of interior modernizations, the exterior woodwork and stonework can't be altered, thus preserving the historical integrity of the site.

Within the home, evidence of historical preservation abounds, such as in the Revolutionary War flintlock used by one of the early Dearing Family residents, and the fireplace andirons imported in 1620, now found in the attached summer kitchen. Irwin is a knowledgeable and enthusiastic guide, pointing out both the authentic, such as the cross-and-Bible patterning found on one door, and the architectural impurity of an arched doorway from a Jeffersonian-inspired renovation.

Even in his present role as innkeeper, I could hear an echo in Phil's voice of his earlier career. He spent 24 years as a radio personality for Voice of America, a position that eventually led him to the Washington, D.C. area. From there he began searching outwards along rivers for a place to purchase. One thing that was important to him was being able to control the view from his home.

Irwin's love of the area is evident when he says, "Rarely have I seen mountains and valleys so perfectly enmeshed." He explains the need to preserve the property with a story of guests whose gaze was captured by an unusual breakfast visitor. As they dined, a bear from Shenandoah National Park climbed the wall near their window, captured an apple, and quietly left with its booty. They playfully wondered how Phil could arrange such a treat for their eyes. While nature is not under his authority, his care for the land allows such natural occurrences to flow unimpeded.

The VOF promotes the preservation of open space lands in part by accepting and holding perpetual conservation easements and holds easements on more than 235,000 acres says the organization's Leslie Grayson.

"These lands are permanently protected by the easements and allow the landowners to enjoy their properties," she says. "An easement provides the landowner with the assurance that the land will remain rural and permits uses that protect the natural resources. Land under easement to the VOF may be sold or passed to heirs, and yet will remain subject to the donor's easement.

"In many cases, easements can be valuable estate planning tools by allowing protected lands to be passed on, with lower taxes, to the next generation. Open space easements benefit everyone by protecting natural resources, watersheds, and scenic vistas while maintaining private ownership of those protected lands."

Grayson concludes that Caledonia "is a county, state, and national treasure." Phil explains that the view from Caledonia Farm is now "guaranteed for the next millennium," but you won't want to wait that long to see it for yourself.

For more information on the VOF, contact the organization at 203 Governor St., Suite 317, Richmond, VA 23219 (804-225-2147), www.virginiaoutdoorsfoundation.com To stay at Caledonia Farm-1812, call 800-BNB-1812, www.bnb-n-va.com/cale1812.htm.

Part Two
The South Fork and Main Stem of the Shenandoah

Shelia and Terry Pleskonko shoving off on the South Fork where the South and North rivers commingle.

2.1
PORT REPUBLIC TO ISLAND FORD

The Essentials

Trip: Confluence of North and South rivers at Port Republic to Island Ford, both in Rockingham County. Refer to Map 1 in Appendix C.

USGS Quads: Grottoes and McGaheysville

Distance: 10 miles

Rapids: Class Is and riffles

Access Points: At the confluence, a dirt/gravel ramp exists on river right off Route 955 via Route 659 and Route 340. Parking spaces exist for twenty-five vehicles. At Island Ford, a dirt/gravel ramp exists on river right off Route 642 via Route 649 and Route 340. Parking is available in a gravel lot.

What a great thrill it is to dip a paddle into the water where a famous river begins. I especially feel this joy on the South Fork of the Shenandoah, as this Northern Virginia stream is rich in history. For example, near the confluence of the North and South rivers, the Battle of Port Republic was fought on June 9, 1862. Here, General Thomas J. "Stonewall" Jackson defeated the Union Army in the Northern Virginia Campaign. Jackson is said to have bowed his head in prayer and raised his right hand toward heaven as the vanquished Northerners retreated. The general was not so lost in prayer, however, as to forgo burning a bridge over the South Fork to keep the Yankee forces from returning. On my maiden Port Republic voyage, I had to ask friends Terry and Shelia Pleskonko of Mt. Sidney to pose for pictures at the put-in, so that I could record the beginnings of the South Fork.

At ten miles, the Port Republic excursion is an all-day affair for both canoeists and float fishermen. This trek is made even longer because of a long portage around a dilapidated dam that lies a little more than two miles into the float. That portage has made the Port Republic section one of the least floated on the South Fork and the Main Stem. As is typical on many Virginia and West Virginia streams, the fishing is quite poor at the put-in. River runners may want to quickly paddle the first one hundred yards or so through a deep, carp-infested pool until they reach a riffle. Below that riffle exists large submerged boulders and plenty of small eddies; this is the initial fishing opportunity on the South Fork.

Next comes a long straight stretch of approximately half a mile. This portion doesn't offer much in the way of fishing, but it is very characteristic of numerous sections of the South Fork. In many places, agricultural fields border the river, and sycamores, silver maples, and box elders thrive along the shorelines. During the warm weather period, expect to see numerous bank swallows flitting about as they catch insects and then take these hapless creatures to their nests. Generations of swallows have reared young in the high dirt walls that flank the river. Also expect to hear or see such avians as house wrens, tufted titmice, common grackles, and the occasional barn swallow here.

Near the one-mile point, you will come to a Class I rapid at what was once known as Jones Island, but now is called Green Island. Actually, Green is not much of an island anymore as the left passageway is almost entirely silted in. According to *The Shenandoah River Atlas*, gundalows used the left channel until 1833. That's when a milldam was constructed at this site, causing the river to flow to the right. The Shenandoah atlas is filled with historical tidbits, and I strongly recommend this publication for history enthusiasts as well as those who desire detailed information about the river and its place names. Information on ordering the atlas can be found in this book's appendix.

The Class I rapid at Green Island takes a hard swing toward river right and often serves as a depository for downed trees and assorted flotsam. Terry Pleskonko recommends that paddlers stay as far as they can to the left side of the Class I in order to avoid that debris. On one trip here with Terry, I lost a fine 3-pound or so smallmouth that mauled a crankbait; it was just a few feet from the canoe. The Shenandoah was rather stained that day (the South River meanders through agricultural fields and often causes the South Fork to become discolored after rain), and I had opted for a chartreuse crankbait because of the lack of water clarity. Generally, I prefer many other lures and fly patterns to crankbaits because the smallmouths often throw these lures, which typically have two sets of treble hooks dangling from their undersides. I don't understand the physics of the matter, but I lose more smallmouths on crankbaits than with any other lure or fly. When the three pounder sounded toward the rocky bottom, I fully expected for the bass to dislodge the crankbait. Sure enough, it did. A better bait in stained water is a 1/4 to 3/8-ounce spinnerbait with a single chartreuse Colorado blade. The lone Colorado blade gives off more vibrations than a willowleaf model, and the chartreuse color is very visible. Also, single hooked lures seem to be better at keeping bass on than artificials with multiple hooks.

After the rushing water below the Class I finally slows, so does the fishing as another long, straight stretch ensues. The scenery is quite fetching, though, and photographers may desire to capture the rural landscape, especially if the sky is azure and the water an emerald green. Several riffles then create aerated water and more fishing opportunities. The next landmark is where Deep Run dribbles in on river right, and soon afterwards you will spot the remains of an old dam on the same

41

side. Not far below this dam another riffle forms. Below this riffle is a marvelous place to beach the boat and work the eddy that metamorphoses on river left. On that same side, you will be able to spot a high bank where bank swallows are sure to be nesting during the warm weather period. Water willow grows along the right side in great profusion.

The next major feature is the Route 708 Bridge near the community of Lynwood at just past the two-mile point. This is an informal access point as you can enter the South Fork on river right below the bridge. I don't recommend accessing the river here if you possess a craft bigger, or heavier, than a canoe. Wade fishermen, though, can enjoy some fair action for smallmouths, rock bass, and redbreast sunfish in this general area. Great masses of dead trees typically are jammed around the bridge, and that wood often harbors fish. A utility wire crosses the river here as well; look for belted kingfishers to be fishing from these lines.

Not far below the Route 708 Bridge, you will espy the piers of the Old Lynwood Bridge on river left. The concrete chunks from that structure pock the stream bottom and create a riffle and some dandy angling. This is yet another place where anglers may want to beach their craft and indulge themselves in wade fishing. Downstream, sycamores thrive along the river left bank, and orchard orioles emit their lilting songs from the treetops. The root wads of those sycamores often harbor jumbo smallmouths. The next major feature is a Class I rapid. This rapid is not at all dangerous, but it is difficult to run because the water is so shallow during the warm water period. You may have to drag your boat down the rapid's right side. Soon afterwards, you will float past a tall cement tower, which apparently used to be a river gauge, on river left. Below the gauge, a river long ledge extends across the South Fork and grass beds grow in great profusion downstream.

The South Fork then forms a river right outside bend, and the stream narrows considerably. Both banks are heavily wooded, and the plaintive whistles of the Eastern wood peewee, which constantly belts out "peewee" with a few peeweeees for variety, are often heard during the late spring and early to mid-summer period. The river then widens and a series of boulders mark the streambed on the right side. Next comes the infamous Big Eddy. This is a long, slow moving section that begins after the four-mile point and continues for more than a mile. The Big Eddy is a grim affair for both fishermen and canoeists as the small-mouth bass are scarce and the current barely detectable. Toward the latter half of the Big Eddy, railroad tracks run along river right, and you will also see a drainage pipe running below the tracks and emptying into the river. About the only fishable areas for smallmouth fans are a few precipitous dropoffs that occur. But since this is such a long float, I recommend paddling non-stop through the Big Eddy.

This slow section finally ends at about the 5½-mile point. An island cleaves the river and water willow grows in abundance; take the left channel for the best fishing and most water. For nearly two miles, a series of riffles continue, and the smallmouth action can be terrific. This is a marvelous stretch for the long rodder to work streamers and Clouser Minnows and for the spinfisherman to employ grubs, buzzbaits, and prop baits. Ospreys are also known to frequent this section, and I once saw this predator capture a small fish here. Inevitably, this aerated water ends as the backwaters of McGaheysville Dam come into play. Redbreast sunfish flourish in this pool as do channel catfish and carp, but the smallmouth fishing is quite poor.

Guide Billy Kingsley of Harrisonburg describes the McGaheysville Dam as a "menace to navigation" and fisheries biologists Steve Reeser and Paul Bugas of the Virginia Department of Game and Inland Fisheries (VDGIF) warn boaters to be very careful in the dam's vicinity. Various floods have dislodged great concrete chunks of the dam, and dangerous hydraulics exist between the dam and various remains of it. Terry Pleskonko recommends that boaters portage around the left side of the dam, but assorted briars and undergrowth grow in monstrous profusion there. Really, there's no good way to portage this dam, and bits and pieces of the dam, some of them quite sharp, seem to be everywhere above and below the structure. Bugas says that the VDGIF would like to see the dam removed, but its fate lies in the hands of the Rockingham County, which owns it. Military demo-lition gangs have conducted test charges, and one possibility is that the military could blow up the remains as part of a training exercise. Con-cerned paddlers may contact the Rockingham County planners to inquire about the dam's current status. As Bugas notes: "It is in everyone's best interest for the dam to be removed."

Usually good fishing exists below dams, but Terry Pleskonko maintains that is not frequently the case downstream from the McGaheysville structure. The angling does pick up, though, when a Class I rapid, which offers numerous passageways, appears. Riffles occur frequently for the rest of this trek. Ledges, wooded shorelines, scattered water willow beds, and, on river left, a white house with impressive columns also characterize the remaining three miles of the Port Republic getaway. After a long day on the river, you will spot the river right Island Ford landing, just above the Route 649 Bridge.

Elaine Ingram with a fine smallmouth taken on the Island Ford float.

2.2
ISLAND FORD TO ELKTON

The Essentials

Trip: Island Ford to Elkton, both in Rockingham County. Refer to Map 1 in Appendix C.

USGS Quads: McGaheysville and Elkton West

Distance: 7 miles

Rapids: Class IIs, Is, and riffles

Access Points: At Island Ford, a dirt/gravel ramp exists on river right off Route 642 via Route 649 and Route 340. Parking is available in a gravel parking lot. At Elkton, a dirt ramp exists on river right off Business Route 33. Wood steps, railings, and a boat slide lead from the ramp. Parking is available in a gravel lot.

Few rivers anywhere in the country have as rich a history as the South Fork of the Shenandoah. In the 1700s, German Lutherans who had traveled southward from Pennsylvania and Maryland settled the northern Shenandoah Valley. Scotch-Irish, mostly of the Presbyterian faith, journeyed eastward across the Atlantic, and through the Blue Ridge Mountains to establish homesteads in the southern reaches of the valley. Others came from England, as was true for the Ingram family. Through genealogical research, I learned that my great, great, great, great grandfather Alexander passed through the Shenandoah Valley in the 1740s before settling in Botetourt County. Many of the settlers from England were Dissenters; they had traveled to America to attain religious freedom. In England, the Church of England, that is the Episcopal Church, controlled religious matters, leading to no separation of church and state. I have often wondered whether Alexander's trek through the Shenandoah Valley was driven by the desire for a better life or to experience religious freedom from an oppressive church/state.

The Island Ford excursion is one of my favorites on the entire Shenandoah system. Canoeists can easily undertake this float in three to four hours while fishermen will need about seven hours, using the standard one mile per hour float plan. Guide Billy Kingsley of Harrisonburg characterizes the Island Ford junket as "being choked with smallmouth bass and containing a few muskies as well," a comment with which I readily agree. The first half-mile of this trip offers only fair fishing and scenery. A grassy left bank and a tree shrouded right shoreline characterize this section, as do patches of curlyleaf pondweed. At one spot on river left, a long, water willow-covered point creates a riffle. Also note that Route 642 parallels the river right shoreline over much of the first half of this float. The first major feature is an island that occurs when a river left bend forms about a half-mile from the put-in. Take the left side of the island for the best route. Near the end of the island, you will spot a Class II rapid that has some triangular shaped rocks studding its heart. That rapid is separated from the river left shoreline by a sand/gravel bar that has a passageway on the left side. If you decide to run this rapid, do so on its left side; the best plan, though, is to veer over to the river left shoreline and take advantage of the passageway. Excellent fishing exists along the island and downstream as well for a mile and a half. Riffles and water willow beds occur with great frequency in this section, and a series of downed trees, especially on river right, create fishing opportunities.

At about the two-mile point, the river starts to narrow, and you will espy another island; the best pathway is on the left. A field and a red-and-white farmhouse on river right help mark this spot. Below the island, scattered riffles occur, but the river slows noticeably at about the three-mile point as the South Fork forms a long, flat river left outside bend. Some deep-water ledges exist and hold both largemouths and smallmouths, but for the most part this is bland, featureless water. Through here, the Merck Company owns the river right shoreline. When the leaves are off the trees, you will be able to see some of the plant buildings, and a few structures are visible throughout the year, including a cylinder shaped one near the river. Scattered fields characterize the river left shoreline. On one journey, I saw the makings of a Norman Rockwell painting along that left bank. A husband, his wife, and their two children, one of whom was in charge of a white poodle, had come to the river from their farmhouse to fish. A Sunday afternoon was in progress and what could be better than the entire family going down to the river to fish and wade. One of the kids yanked a sunfish from the South Fork, and the prime ingredient for a fish fry was put into a cooler. The simple joys of life still have meaning today.

The South Fork then narrows considerably and riffles begin to form. Several of those riffles may metamorphose into Class I rapids when water levels are high. On one trip with my wife Elaine and Billy Kingsley, I scored by working the river right shoreline where sycamores have grown in great profusion. Sycamores are magnets for smallmouth bass as their leafy canopies create shade, and their extensive root systems provide ambush points along the bank. On that getaway, I tossed a 4-inch Venom tube bait to one of those sycamore root wads and was rewarded with an 18-inch bronzeback. Later along another sycamore dominated shoreline, I corralled a 16-incher that fell for a 6-inch Mister Twister worm, once again proving that the root pattern can be a big bass one. Kingsley, who specializes in flyfishing, likes to cast crayfish patterns and streamers to this type of cover.

At about the 4½-mile point, Hawksbill Creek enters on river right. The river then takes a sharp bend to the left, and soon you will see a gorgeous river left bluff. This is certainly one of the more pictur-esque locales of the Island Ford trek, and photography enthusiasts may want to practice their craft here. The smallmouth action can also be outstanding as deep-water rocks and dropoffs characterize the left shoreline. Below the rock bluff, the river narrows and an island dots the river. The left side offers the best passageway and enticing fishing as well. Be sure to target the water willow beds with Sneaky Pete Pop-pers, hair bugs, Heddon Tiny Torpedos, and Rebel Pop'Rs. Riffles exist throughout the passageway and can be found below the island as well. Then you will come to another island, which creates riffles and marvel-ous fishing.

The next major feature is Merck Park on river right. The park allows hand carry canoe access. The simplest way to access the river is from Route 1709 via Route 634. Route 1709 dead ends at some rail-road tracks, and you can carry your canoe across the tracks to the river. Parking is very limited on Route 1709. You can also enter the park by going down a series of suburban streets to reach a shelter; parking spaces are numerous. No formal access point exists; you merely slide your canoe across some grass into the river. Merck Park is easily visible from the river, and a series of riffles help mark the location. Within sight of the shelter is a Class II rapid. During several floats through this area, I have experimented with how to run this Class II. You can dodge some medicine ball size rocks in the middle and on river left, or you can take a shallow run on far river left and avoid all the rocks. I recommend the latter option. In any event, some superb micro-eddies exist below the Class II, and the shaded river right bank offers additional opportunities. You may also want to note the river left bank; sandpits exist there.

Immediately downstream, after a series of riffles, lies a railroad bridge. These structures are among the most scenic on rivers, and almost always I stop to take color slides of them. A deep pool forms below the tracks and is a popular destination for catfish anglers. The same description rings true for the Route 33 Bridge, which spans the South Fork. A beautiful river left bluff also marks this area. Next ensues a Class I rapid and some riffles. The Route 33 Business Bridge marks the river right take-out and the conclusion of one of the South Fork's premier floats.

The Elkton excursion is a marvelous for canoeists and anglers.

2.3
ELKTON TO SHENANDOAH

The Essentials

Trip: Elkton to Shenandoah, both in Rockingham County. Refer to Map 2 in Appendix C.

USGS Quads: Elkton West and Elkton East

Distance: 7 miles

Rapids: Class Is and riffles

Access Points: At Elkton, a dirt ramp exists on river right off Business Route 33. Wood steps, railings, and a boat slide lead from the ramp. Parking is available in a gravel lot. At Shenandoah, a concrete ramp exists on river right off Route 602 (Maryland Avenue) via Route 340. Parking spaces are numerous in the gravel lot.

One of America's great presidents was a son of the Shenandoah Valley. Born in Staunton, Virginia in 1856, Woodrow Wilson became the 28th president in 1913 and served two terms. An educational place to visit in the Shenandoah Valley is Wilson's boyhood home in Staunton. Highlights include guided tours of family heirlooms and period furnishings, as well as the opportunity to gain insight into the man who was commander in chief of America's forces in World War I. He helped craft the Versailles Treaty ending the conflict.

The Elkton trip is a pleasant afternoon getaway for paddlers and an all day journey for float fishermen, and the latter category of outdoorsmen don't have to wait long to enjoy the action. A rocky pool exists below the Route 33 Business Bridge, and I began one trip by catching a 17-inch smallmouth here on a 4-inch tube. Interestingly, a sewage disposal outflow (the water has been treated) enters on river right below the bridge, but the fishing is none the worse for this release.

The rest of the first mile or so of the Elkton junket features the occasional riffle and rows of sycamores, especially on river left. Biologist Steve Reeser relates that this section often harbors some hand-size panfish. Indeed, the sunfish clan is well represented in the South Fork, he says, as rock bass, bluegills, and redbreast, pumpkinseed, and green sunfish all dwell in the river. Reeser adds that the state occasionally stocks muskies, usually when a surplus of this species has occurred at a hatchery. Largemouth bass also live in the South Fork, and I have seen bucketmouths over five pounds caught. Reeser says that the biggest largemouth he has heard taken from the river is seven pounds.

Near the two-mile point, the South Fork forms a slight, river right outside bend. Generally, this arm of the Shenandoah is not a river characterized by sharp outside bends. This is one of the older streams in the two Virginias, and over the centuries these bends have gradually straightened. This is in contrast to a younger stream, such as the James River, where the outside bends are often relatively sharp and horseshoe shaped. On the South Fork, the horseshoes have become more elongated. As the bend concludes, you will espy Needle Rock, which looks like a more than 6-foot-tall arrowhead anchored to the river right bottom. Just below Needle Rock several small islands appear; take the right passageway for the best fishing and easiest paddling. Terry

Pleskonko and I once stopped here to do some wade fishing. Terry began to catch good size bronzebacks on tubes while I scored with Berkley Frenzy poppers. Armed with the knowledge that the bass would hit on the bottom and surface, we alternated between those two baits the rest of the day and caught and released more than a dozen smallies between 12 and 17 inches. I always find it a good idea for a boating partner and myself to use different lures and fly imitations at least at the start of a trip. Then if one individual ascertains what the bass are hitting, both people can share in the success. If you and your boatmate are employing the same imitations, determining the pattern can take much longer.

After the islands, the South Fork flows straight for more than half a mile. Boone Run, also known as Lick Run, enters on river left at about the three-mile point of the float. And below this small tributary, you will see a utility wire crossing the river, as well as possibly some bank swallows, which like to perch on it. This section offers satisfying angling as a rocky bottom predominates and riffles often form. The only drawback of this area is that I often see cows cooling themselves in the waterway. Bovines are a terrible source of pollution and their stomping down of the banks causes erosion and sedimentation. A good investment for any state would be to create watering holes for cattle and streamside fencing along shorelines to keep livestock out of a river. Our streams would be much healthier, and so would the estuaries and bays that they flow into. Unfortunately, many states are pennywise and pound-foolish on this matter.

At about the halfway mark of the Elkton float, the South Fork creates a river left bend and a Class I rapid. The best passageway is down the river left side, which offers a clear chute. I once saw two novice paddlers try the river right path, and they capsized about half way down. Any rapid can cause problems, and paddlers should always look over any swift water section before entering it. Superlative smallie sport exists below this rapid. I like to position my canoe so that it floats vertically to both shorelines. That way, my journey downstream is slowed, and I can thoroughly work likely areas. For the next mile or so, the river flows at a fair pace, just fast enough to keep paddlers engaged and just aerated enough to cause the mossybacks to be active. This is a

51

wonderful stretch to toss hair bugs and poppers as well as surface lures such as Jitterbugs and Storm Chug Bugs. Look for overhanging trees that shade several square yards of the river. If the water beneath those trees is a foot or more deep, good size smallmouths may be lurking and will likely maul a surface imitation.

At about the five-mile point, an easy Class I rapid looms and a riffle follows. Both are fairly shallow and the fishing is only average. The safest path through the rapid is on river right. Next comes Dido Rocks, a series of huge bluffs on river right. These bluffs are stunningly beautiful and a recommended stop for photographers. A sheep farm exists on river left, and you can beach your boat in the shallows to take photos. A deep pool borders the bluffs, and on a sunny day, you may be able to capture the reflection of Dido Rocks in the water. The slow water continues below Dido Rocks, and the angling is poor, unless you are after muskies or channel catfish.

Smallmouth fishing opportunities are rare for the rest of this trip. At about the six-mile mark, another long pool metamorphoses. Numerous river right bluffs punctuate the shoreline, which create numerous photo opportunities. Below these bluffs, a riffle forms; this is the last place I wet a line on the Elkton excursion. This is because the backwaters of Shenandoah Dam create a power pool. A twenty-minute or so paddle will then take you to the river right take-out (a fishing dock helps mark the access point) and the termination of the Elkton float. A series of red buoys strung across the river warn of the impending dam.

Shenandoah to Grove Hill offers outstanding scenery, paddling, and fishing.

2.4
SHENANDOAH TO GROVE HILL

The Essentials

Trip: Shenandoah in Rockingham County to Grove Hill in Page County. Refer to Map 2 in Appendix C.

USGS Quads: Elkton West, Elkton East, Tenth Legion, and Stanley

Distance: 8 miles

Rapids: Class IIs, Is, and riffles

Access Points: Below Shenandoah Dam, a river right dirt ramp exists off Route 1017 (Long Avenue) via Route 602 (Maryland Avenue) and Route 340. Parking is very limited. To reach the ramp, turn off Route 1017 at a cream-colored brick building and drive down a gravel path to the river. At Grove Hill, a gravel ramp exists on river right off Route 650 via Route 340. Parking spaces are numerous in a gravel lot.

On one float down the South Fork, Terry Pleskonko and I gave a Mennonite man a lift to his car. While riding, I asked him about the history of his branch of Protestants in the Shenandoah Valley. Many Mennonites originally settled in the valley when they journeyed southward from Pennsylvania. The ones who remained in the Keystone State are often known as Amish, which is an offshoot of the Mennonites. Both groups tend to emphasize living and dressing simply and are among the Protestant faiths that stress the New Testament. Traditionally, Mennonites have been opposed to war or swearing oaths. Today, this faith often engages in rural pastimes such as dairy farming, cattle rearing, and the raising of various crops; its members are a credit to the entire Shenandoah Valley.

Paddlers can easily accomplish the Shenandoah junket in four hours while float fishermen will want to allot the better part of the day. Anglers should note that this trip marks the beginning of the 14- to 20-inch slot limit on the South Fork. From the base of the Shenandoah Dam downstream to Luray Dam, 14 to 20 inch bass may not be creeled, and only one fish longer than 20 inches may be kept per day. This regulation went into effect on January 1, 2001. Upstream from Shenandoah Dam to the beginnings of the South Fork at Port Republic, the longstanding 11- to 14-inch slot limit is in effect. The 11- to 14-inch slot goes back into effect from the base of Luray Dam to the confluence of the North and South Forks of the Shenandoah at Front Royal. A five-bass limit is in effect on the slot sections. Biologist Steve Reeser told me that a goal of the 14- to 20-inch slot is to protect bass in that size range so that they can be caught and released more than once, thus providing angling pleasure for a number of sportsmen. On the Shenandoah system, smallmouths more than 20 inches are much less common than they are on the James and New.

Upon launching, anglers may want to paddle upstream and fish the tailrace below Shenandoah Dam. This is also a good place for wade fishermen to access the river. Always be sure to wear a lifejacket while wading, especially below dams where the current is often swift. At the launch site, an island cleaves the South Fork. The most water lies to the left of the island, but there is also a tricky Class II rapid. Logs and other debris tend to collect on the left side of the rapid and a series of ledges exist as well; portage on the right side of the rapid, next to the island. You may have to drag your canoe through part of the right passageway along the island, but this route is much safer. Below the island, be prepared for some excellent scenery and fishing. Several bluffs mark the river left bank, and the heavily wooded shoreline creates a pleasing vista. Photographers will want to take advantage of this opportunity.

People often ask whether I shoot slides or prints. Magazines prefer color slides, so all of my pictures are taken with that category of film. I favor Kodachrome 64 because I believe the colors of that brand are the truest to nature. However, many professional photographers opt for Fujichrome 50 or 100, and other camera enthusiasts have their favorites as well. Others use one brand for one type of situation while selecting another for a different application. Generally, Kodachrome excels at capturing reds, oranges, and yellows while Fujichrome is well known for its ability to reproduce vivid blues and greens. The bluffs and background along river left are so photogenic, that it would be hard not to depict their allure. And the fishing is quite good as well.

As you travel downstream, you will note an out-flow, a concrete block, and some bluffs on river right. A power line also crosses the river in this area. On one float, my wife Elaine and I stopped to talk to two elderly gentlemen who were angling for carp in the slow moving pool. They proudly raised an 8-pound carp that they had caught while dunking a doughball. Carp are probably the most scorned fish on the river, but their brute size and dogged nature makes them great battlers. And as one of the two gents informed me: "Carp roe tastes like caviar." In any event, carp in the 5- to 12-pound range fin the slow moving sections of the entire Shenandoah system.

Just before the one-mile point, you will come to what is sometimes known as Schuler Island. Upstream, a series of sycamore trees line the river right bank and provide shaded sanctuaries to smallmouths, rock bass, and redbreast sunfish. Take the right passageway past Schuler. Shortly afterwards, you will see another island; journey down its left side. Usually good fishing exists downstream from islands, but in the case of the latter island mentioned above, the river is very shallow and pebble-dominated, although the islet itself and the wooded banks are very scenic. Next you will see two sets of power lines as the river begins a two-mile-long horseshoe bend. This bend has very shallow water of only a few feet, and a forest blankets much of the river left shoreline. Halfway through the bend, you will encounter an island; take the right pathway. Although the fishing is only mediocre through here, waterfowl are abundant. On one float, Elaine and I watched a wood duck shepherding her young, and mallards and Canada geese also dwell here. Another power line and a river left silo tell you that you are nearing the end of the bend and approaching the three-mile point of the Shenandoah excursion.

Next comes another island; travel down its left side. And several hundred yards later, you will arrive at a much larger island. The best route is around the right side, and an easy Class I lies near the end. I like to stop and rest here and do some wade fishing. Water willow beds grow along the island and several ledges and dropoffs attract smallies. The next major feature is a riffle, followed shortly afterwards by a power line, which together mark the four-mile point and the beginning of the most pleasing portion of the Shenandoah trek. Up to this point, the smallmouth action has been spotty, but for the next two miles expect outstanding bassing and superlative scenery. The George Washington and Jefferson National Forest dominates the river left shoreline as the river makes a horseshoe bend. The mountainous left bank harbors vireos, warblers, hawks, and ospreys; and riffles pock the river through-out. One Class I rapid exists at about the midway point where three islands cleave the stream; take the middle passageway for the most water. Consider budgeting several hours for this section if you are an angler, bird watcher, nature lover, or photographer. I like to flyfish with Sneaky Pete poppers and damselfly imitations through here as the bass frequently feed on the surface. I also once caught a nearly 20-inch bronzeback on a twin-tail grub that I had tossed beneath an overhanging tree. This entire river left outside bend harbors big bass.

A power line marks the approximate end of the outside bend and soon you will see fields on river left and homes along the right shoreline. Next comes the Kite's Ford area, which is characterized by shallow runs and riffles and only average angling. The exception is a Class I-II rapid which features a sharp drop on far river right. I recommend running this rapid on far river left for a very easy passageway. Yet another power line then crosses the river, as does Route 340; you will also be able to hear the sounds of traffic coming from Route 650, which runs along river right.

The last mile of this float offers very poor bass fishing. Scattered water willow beds dot the streambed as do numerous small riffles. At the beginning of this section, a Class I rapid appears to the right of one islet, but several passageways exist or you can venture down the shallow left side. The Grove Hill Landing on river right concludes a very interesting float.

The Grove Hill junket provides pleasing vistas like this one.

2.5
GROVE HILL TO NEWPORT

The Essentials

Trip: Grove Hill to Newport, both in Page County. Refer to Map 3 in Appendix C.

USGS Quad: Stanley

Distance: 6 miles

Rapids: Class II rapid and riffles

Access Points: At Grove Hill, a gravel ramp exists on river right off Route 650 via Route 340. Parking spaces are numerous in a gravel lot. At Newport, a dirt ramp exists on river left off Route 340. The ramp is quite steep, and the launching of motorized craft is not recommended. Parking is available in a dirt/gravel lot.

Before or after the Grove Hill float, you may want to visit the Hall of Valor Civil War Museum at New Market Battlefield State Park. The museum's highlight is its depiction of the 257 Virginia Military Institute college boys. These brave lads suffered terrible losses as they dueled with Union forces on May 15, 1864. The museum is at the site of the Jacob Bushong farm, where the battle raged. The farmstead offers displays from the battle as well as insight into mid-nineteenth century Shenandoah Valley farm life.

A crucial aspect of writing a river guide is for the author to be honest. In all honesty, then, I rate the Grove Hill trip as, at best, mediocre. For paddlers, the Grove Hill junket must be rated as poor. Massanutten Dam interrupts the trip at around the four-mile point, necessitating a long (at least twenty minutes) and unpleasant river right portage. Float fishermen will find the smallmouth action only fair and certainly not comparable to the sport that exists on many other sections. However, muskie and channel catfish fans will like this junket because of the deep, slow pools. Factoring in the portage, canoeists should be able to negotiate this trip in three hours. Due to the lack of bass habitat, smallmouth anglers will need only an hour or so more than canoeists to cover the best spots.

Soon after launching, you will pass under a powerline and through several shallow riffles. Except for the spring period, shallow is the operative word for the first two miles of the Grove Hill trip. Elodea, star grass, curlyleaf pondweed, and Eurasian milfoil grow in such profusion that vegetation chokes the river, making paddling difficult in places and retrieving a fly or lure frustrating. Normally, riffles are a boon to paddlers and anglers, but on this float they have so little depth that a canoe often scrapes the bottom and the bass have nowhere to seek sanctuary. Route 650 parallels the stream on river right for the first two miles, and assorted homes and trailers dot the shoreline. The scenery is just as lacking as the paddling and fishing, although the river left bank is mostly wooded.

At about the two-mile point, a bluff looms on river left and a powerline crosses the river. A deep pool forms here, and for the next two miles, water will continue to be backed up because of Massanutten Dam, also known as the Newport Dam and Hydro Plant. These two miles can easily be summarized as follows. Just downstream from the powerline, Hickory Run enters on river right and a half mile or so later, Baten Rocks dominates the river left shoreline. This is actually a very scenic spot, and photographers may want to capture Baten's reflection in the pool below. At the three-mile point, Acheron Rocks looms on river right. Acheron Rocks is a series of gorgeous bluffs, and George Washington is supposed to have carved his initials on one of them. On one trip with the fishing being poor, frequent fishing buddy Terry Pleskonko and I decided to search for Washington's initials. Alas, all we found was "Ron loves Kim" spray-painted at the base of one bluff.

Another half mile of paddling will take you to a private ramp owned by Dam Acres Campground, which lies on the river right bank of the power pool. Unless you have paid a fee to the campground, you may not use this ramp. Actually, you can have a shorter portage if you paddle approximately fifty yards further and take out just above the red buoys, signifying that the easily visible Massanutten Dam is near. (Neroe Rocks on river left also distinguishes the dam area.) This trail is the state designated portage path. You will have to haul your craft up a bank and along a track, then down another bank below the dam. If you would rather not take the first four miles of this float, you can access the river by means of Route 617 (Dam Acres Road) via Route 650.

Below the dam, the fishing and scenery immediately improve. Be careful immediately below the dam because jagged concrete slabs and exposed metal rods from a previous dam exist in a number of places. A bluff adds beauty to the river right shoreline; riffles, ledges, and boulders provide excellent cover for smallmouths. A half-mile later, you will come to the remains of Newport Mill, a combined sawmill and gristmill on river left. A Class II rapid punctuates the river here and features a 6-foot drop. The rapid has a strong hydraulic at its base, and I recommend that paddlers portage on river right. An island lies to the left of the rapid, but do not go to the left of the island to avoid the rapid. The pathway is very shallow and remains of the mill clog the channel, which is extremely narrow. Shortly afterwards, you will arrive at the river left Newport take-out.

Terry Pleskonko with a fine smallie taken on the Newport trip.

2.6
NEWPORT TO ALMA

The Essentials
Trip: Newport to Alma, both in Page County. Refer to Map 3 in Appendix C.

USGS Quad: Stanley

Distance: 3 miles

Rapids: Class I Columbian Falls and riffles

Access Points: At Newport, a dirt ramp exists on river left off Route 340. The ramp is quite steep, and the launching of motorized craft is not recommended. Parking is available in a dirt/gravel lot. At Alma, a dirt/gravel ramp exists on river right under the Route 340 Business Bridge. Parking spaces are numerous in the gravel lot.

One of the most pleasant aspects of venturing forth on just about any trip down the South Fork of the Shenandoah is floating by the many farms that line the river. Although the Shenandoah Valley, like many parts of Virginia, has experienced considerable population growth in recent decades, much of the region still retains its rural ambience, and farming is a major part of everyday life. During the Civil War, in fact, the Shenandoah Valley was known as the "breadbasket of the Confederacy." Both the North and South knew well the importance of the valley to the Confederacy's survival, and that is why, in part, the region was the site of so many battles. Some historians believe a major blow to the South's chances took place in 1864 when General Ulysses S. Grant ordered General Philip Sheridan to eliminate agriculture in the valley "so that a crow flying over it will have to carry his provender with him." Sheridan succeeded in carrying out Grant's orders and the South's surrender came the following year.

The Newport getaway is a delight for outdoor enthusiasts of all persuasions. Paddlers will be able to travel the three miles in little more than an hour but may want to linger among the many water willow covered islets. Float fishermen can easily spend an entire afternoon on this section of the South Fork. Long rodders will especially relish this junket because it is tailor-made for wade fishing and casting popping and hair bugs. And photographers will enjoy capturing the braided channels, wooded hillsides, and surrounding bucolic countryside on film.

Soon after launching you will espy Pyramid Rocks on river left. This bluff marks a great place to angle for smallmouths as submerged rocks litter the stream bottom. Actually, the entire river left, nearly one-mile-long outside bend that Pyramid Rocks looks over proffers fine fishing as gentle riffles and submerged rock characterize this section. Fly fishermen should try weighted Clouser minnows and streamers while spinfishermen can run spinnerbaits and soft plastic baits through the depths. At about the one-mile point, Columbian Falls begins. This section endures for approximately one-fifth of a mile and provides marvelous mossyback sport. The scenery is also fetching as both shorelines are heavily wooded. Riffles predominate at the beginning of the falls and an easy Class I rapid concludes it. Throughout, water willow-covered islets provide sanctuaries for a host of creatures. Water willow is truly a remarkable plant, thriving in transitional areas between water and land. Damsel and dragonflies often use the vegetation to rest on and waterfowl, herons, redwing blackbirds, Louisiana waterthrushes, and spotted sandpipers are among the avians that frequent the area. Minnows, crayfish, and hellgrammites thrive along the fringes of the beds, and smallmouths are well aware of this fact. Around water willow beds, I like to toss Sneaky Pete poppers, Heddon Tiny Torpedoes, Rebel Pop'Rs, and Rapala Skitter Pops and Props. A buzzbait is a great choice for bigger bronzebacks.

The fishing remains excellent after Columbian Falls terminates. A series of deep-water ledges dot the bottom for less than half a mile until Silver Falls begins at about the two-mile point. Silver Falls is nothing more than a riffle during the summer, and the braided channel that begins here continues for most of the remaining trip. Riffles are almost non-stop, as is the action for smallmouth bass. Use the same flies and lures recommended for the Columbian Falls section. With about a half-mile left in the float, you will spot the Route 340 Business Bridge at Alma. The fishing and floating fun continue until the bridge, which ends this short but pleasing trip.

Redbreast sunfish are a popular gamefish on the Alma getaway.

2.7
ALMA TO WHITE HOUSE

The Essentials

Trip: Alma to White House, both in Page County. Refer to Map 3 in Appendix C.

USGS Quads: Stanley and Hamburg

Distance: 6 miles

Rapids: Riffles

Access Points: At Alma, a dirt/gravel ramp exists on river right under the Route 340 Business Bridge. Parking spaces are numerous in the gravel parking lot. At White House, a river right concrete ramp exists off Route 646 (Kauffmans Mill Road) via Route 211. The take-out is at the Route 211 Bridge. Parking spaces are numerous in the gravel lot.

One of the most interesting aspects concerning the history of the Shenandoah Valley is the story of the gundalows. Gundalows were wide, flat-bottomed boats up to approximately 20 feet long, and were used to carry goods down the Shenandoah during the nineteenth century. After arriving at their destination, these craft were sold and their lumber turned into buildings. I have often wondered why the gundalows were designed only to go down the Shenandoah system, while the batteau — which were employed on the James during the same time period — traveled upstream and down. Batteau were more streamlined than gundalows, which had a more blunt shape at their bows and sterns. One thing that both craft had in common was that piloting them was often difficult and potentially dangerous. Imagine being in charge of a large, unresponsive craft filled with goods and then having to run a Class II rapid like the ones that punctuate the James and Shenandoah.

The Alma getaway makes for a three or four-hour excursion for paddlers and a day trip of approximately six or so hours for float fishermen. Avid smallmouth angler Craig Fields, who hails from Dumfries, raves that this float is "full of quality smallmouths." Given the gentle nature of the Alma run, I rate it as a great couples float. Birdwatchers will also enjoy a day on the water, as the orchard orioles, among other avians, will serenade them along.

The first mile sets the tone for most of the trip. The river left shoreline is heavily wooded while pastureland characterizes much of the river right bank. Small ledges and gentle riffles provide plenty of places to fish. The largest ledge comes at about the one-mile point, but even this one is only a riffle. Shortly afterwards, an island comes into view; take the left passageway. A wing dam lies in the vicinity of this island, but it too only creates a riffle. I am often asked what are some good flies and lures throughout the warm weather period, especially when riffles and Class I rapids are common. Tom Sadler, who operates the Two Dogs Trading Company guide service in The Plains, Virginia, employs several patterns from spring through fall. He works size 6 to 8 Clouser minnows around deep-water ledges, size 8 to 12 hellgrammites through riffles, and size 6 to 8 Wooly Buggers anywhere a hint of current exists.

By the two-mile point, you will be in the heart of a river left bend. Both shorelines are heavily wooded, and the river left bank offers the most cover for smallmouths. Then a very shallow stretch ensues, which is followed by another island; take the right passageway. This is a very scenic area and a must stop for photographers. Below the island, a series of riffles and ledges occur and offer more angling opportunities. Spin fishermen will want to employ fast moving lures such as grubs, crankbaits, and spinnerbaits as the bass can be quite active.

Next, the river takes a slight curve to the right. Here, according to the *Shenandoah River Atlas*, was the site for Massanutten Mills, a gristmill on the right bank. Only a riffle remains to mark the location. Indeed, the riffle is indistinguishable from all the other riffles that occur in the curve. As the curve straightens, small cliffs line the river right shoreline and offer more photogenic scenery. Just past the 4½ -mile point, Big Run enters on river left and then an island cleaves the South Fork. An attractive wood house rests on the river right bank, further marking the area. Take the left route around the island. Soon you will come to another island; scoot around it on the right side. After you pass by the island, a straight stretch ensues, and the Route 211 Bridge comes into view. Consider taking a slide of the river, the Route 211 Bridge, and the mountain behind. A short paddle will end the Alma float on the South Fork.

The White House float contains plenty of riffles.

2.8
WHITE HOUSE TO MASSANUTTEN

The Essentials

Trip: White House to Massanutten, both in Page County. Refer to Map
4 in Appendix C.

USGS Quad: Hamburg

Distance: 3 miles

Rapids: Riffles

Access Points: At White House, a river right concrete ramp exists off
Route 646 (Kauffmans Mill Road) via Route 211. The put-in is
at the Route 211 Bridge. Parking spaces are numerous in the
gravel lot. At Massanutten, a river left concrete ramp exists off
Route 615 (Egypt Bend Road) by means of Route 211. Parking
is available in a gravel lot.

Wars that end in defeat can leave some generals with negative reputations, sometimes deserved, sometimes not. Consider the case of the South's General Jubal Anderson Early who was largely reviled in Dixie from the time the Civil War ended until his death in 1894. Early opposed secession from the Union, but that transgression was minor compared to later events. Early tried and failed to take Washington, D.C. in July 1864 and then retreated to the Shenandoah Valley, where he suffered even greater ignominy. There, the North's General Phillip H. Sheridan soundly trounced Early in March 1865, helping lead to the eventual defeat of Dixie and fixing Early's reputation in the minds of Southerners. Was Early an incompetent leader or was he fighting battles that no general could have won? Interestingly, Early grew up in Franklin County, Virginia and practiced law there in Rocky Mount. My great-great grandfather James lived in Franklin at the same time, and I can't help but wonder if their paths met.

Anglers and paddlers alike will need only a few hours to traverse this section of the South Fork. Good smallmouth action only exists in the first mile of the float; the rest of the trip consists of flat water best left to those who favor angling for carp and catfish. Although the White House getaway does provide some nice scenery, primarily in the form of bluffs, the sluggish pace of the river greatly lessens the joy of viewing the rock structures.

After the put-in, you will immediately be presented with a decision to take the left or right route around an island. The left passageway, though a riffle, is shallow and typically clogged with debris, making the right path the only option. After you do so, prepare to enjoy some enticing fishing over the next mile or so. A long river left bend forms, and riffles liberally dot the stream. Rocky cover is abundant, making crawfish patterns a good option for long rodders and tube baits the choice for spinfishermen. Friend Craig Fields says this part of the river holds "more 15-inch-plus smallmouths than any stretch I know."

This section basically ends where a riffle forms just upstream from a powerline. This riffle was the site of Strickler's Mill, which operated from the 1820s to 1936 when the waterwheel washed away. Next comes Egypt Bend, which endures for the final two miles of the White House float. Craig Fields and Terry Pleskonko of Mt. Sidney both use the term *"awful flat water"* when describing Egypt Bend, a portrayal that is unfortunately all too accurate. Some small bluffs on river right in the first mile of the bend and Graybeard's Rocks in the second mile are nice to view and photograph, but they alone can not mask the fact that river runners will have to endure considerable paddling to take advantage of the take-out. Numerous docks and homes line the river left shoreline, and paddlers will have to contend with water skiers and pleasure boaters during the summer. A powerline and more docks come into view near the end of the float, and at long last, you will espy the river left ramp. The White House getaway offers a few charms, but it is not one that anglers or paddlers will want to take regularly.

The Massanutten getaway provides some scenic vistas below the dam that interrupts the float.

2.9
MASSANUTTEN TO BIXLERS BRIDGE

The Essentials

Trip: Massanutten to Bixlers Bridge, both in Page County. Refer to Map 4 in Appendix C.

USGS Quads: Hamburg and Luray

Distance: 4 miles

Rapids: Riffles

Access Points: At Massanutten, a river left concrete ramp exists off Route 615 (Egypt Bend Road) by means of Route 211. Parking is available in a gravel lot. At Bixlers Bridge, a river left concrete ramp (known as the Inskeep ramp) exists off Route 675 (Bixlers Ferry Road) where it intersects with Route 684 (Page Valley Road). The ramp can be reached via Route 652 (Airport Road) and Route 211. Although the ramp is concrete, it stops a foot above the stream, making it difficult for trailers to access the river. Parking spaces are numerous in the gravel lot.

One of the most fascinating aspects of life in the pre-twentieth century Shenandoah Valley was the role that apples played in every day life. Apples were the most essential fruit and constituted a major part of a family's diet throughout the year; in fact, they were truly subsistence fare. Families raised different apple varieties that had different culinary purposes and were known to ripen from early to mid-summer until mid-fall. For example, the Yellow Transparent is marvelous as a cooking apple and ripens in early summer. The Summer Rambo shares the same trait, yet ripens later in the summer. Originating in France in the mid-1600s, the Summer Rambo was such a favorite that early settlers brought seedlings with them when they crossed the Atlantic.

Other varieties were favored for their different attributes. The Horse apple matures in early fall and is famous as a drying apple. The Grimes Golden, which originated in West Virginia, is known for making good apple butter. And the Black Twig, my personal favorite, is a superior keeping apple that rural folk could store until well into the spring. The Black Twig also ripens late, usually in late October, and makes mouth-watering pies. Not only did rural residents find these varieties practical, but they also cherished their taste. The truth is that these and other old fashioned varieties are far superior to modern ones such as the Red Delicious, which I feel tastes like moist cardboard. If today's apple consumers knew what the Shenandoah Valley residents of yore knew about apple taste and culture, they would not stand for the modern varieties. Given the public's ignorance concerning apples, the local supermarket would not sell many apples of a variety with a name like Horse, when consumers can buy a bright red, though insipid tasting, Red Delicious.

To be honest, I have taken the Massanutten float twice, and I will never take it again. I rate it as by far the worst trip on the entire South Fork, and one that is lacking in just about every regard. And it contains one of the worst portages of any trip I have ever taken on any river. Not counting portage time, paddlers will only need two or fewer hours to negotiate this trip and anglers will need just an hour or so more.

The float begins in the backwaters of the Luray Hydropower Dam, and for nearly two miles you will have to paddle through this pool. The river right bank is heavily wooded while docks and homes line much of the left side. Red buoys and the power plant itself, on river right, mark the dam; a river left concrete ramp lies just above the buoys. Unfortunately, there is no legal way to portage around the dam. No trespassing signs line the left shoreline. On a float with Terry Pleskonko, we luckily encountered a landowner who kindly helped us portage my Dagger Legend across his property and down a steep, boulder-lined bank to the river below the dam. The rocks are rather jagged, and the bank itself is replete with briers, stinging nettles, and poison oak.

The spillway below the dam receives a great deal of fishing pressure, but I don't understand why. The river bottom is scoured and featureless. Braided channels mercifully lie below the dam and quickly send you away from the area. The remaining mile of the float offers little. A powerline crosses the river at the beginning and some rocky pools dot the river at the end. Also at the end of the float, you will have to undergo one more travail. A low water bridge crosses the South Fork right above the take-out and hard below Bixlers Bridge. The low water bridge is clogged with debris and impossible to float under. The portage on river left is adjacent to the parking lot at the take-out.

Terry Pleskonko working a pool on the Bixlers Bridge float.

2.10
BIXLERS BRIDGE TO FOSTER'S

The Essentials

Trip: Bixlers Bridge to Foster's, both in Page County. Refer to Map 4 in Appendix C.

USGS Quads: Hamburg, Luray, and Rileyville

Distance: 9 miles

Rapids: Class Is and riffles

Access Points: At Bixlers Bridge, a river left concrete ramp (known as the Inskeep ramp) exists off Route 675 (Bixlers Ferry Road) where it intersects with Route 684 (Page Valley Road). The ramp can be reached via Route 652 (Airport Road) and Route 211. Although the ramp is concrete, it stops a foot above the stream, making it difficult for trailers to access the river. Parking spaces are numerous in the gravel lot. At Foster's, a river left concrete ramp exists off Route 684, which is now a gravel road. This ramp also stops a foot above the streambed. Parking spaces are numerous in the gravel lot.

One of the most prominent organizations that strives to keep the history of river travel alive is the Virginia Canals and Navigations Society. A major function of the group is to publish atlases of the major waterways of the state such as the James, Rappahannock, and Shenandoah. Stream travelers of the 1700s and 1800s created river guides that named every rapid and major feature along a river. The descriptions made by these long ago river voyagers are so accurate that modern day paddlers, and this writer, still rely upon them to negotiate rapids and note landmarks. For example, for the Bixlers Bridge float, *The Shenandoah River Atlas* details place names as well as giving tidbits of history. One such tidbit involves the history of Good's Valley Mill, which was operated in the 1830s. Although these descriptions of the river are not totally accurate given the passage of time and the destructive forces of rapids and high water, the atlases are still very reliable and well worth their cost. For more information on the VC&NS and its various river guides, see this book's index.

Anglers will want to allot a full day to the Bixlers Bridge float while canoeists should plan on a half-day excursion. Birdwatchers and photographers will relish this getaway as it is very scenic and avians abound. My wife Elaine and I first took the Bixlers Bridge float a number of years ago with Christian Goebel and his wife Angela. Christian, who operates Shenandoah River Outfitters in Luray, has lived on the river much of his life and is a passionate advocate for the stream. I still recall Angela seining for minnows at the take-out and later Christian snorkeling for madtoms, which he caught with his hands. Christian regards mad toms as the premier live bait for good size smallmouths, and I have seen him catch a number of quality bass that fell for this member of the catfish family.

The first mile of this float is the only uninteresting section. Shallow pools characterize this mile, and a rock bluff on river right and a small rock garden at the end of the mile are the only features worth noting. In the second mile, homes lie along the river left shoreline. The river right shoreline (which is a high bank) hosts mature timber, and a Class I rapid appears. This is the Mill Dam Rapids, which occurs at a small island. You can see some steel reinforcing rods at the bottom of the island, which lies on the left side of the river. Because of the rods, do not take the path down the river left shoreline. Over the next mile, a series of ledges ensue; these ledges and the riffles that form are known as Keysers Falls, although the stream bed does not drop a great deal. All of these ledges and riffles provide quality angling for smallmouths. A powerline concludes this section.

Hawksbill Creek then enters on river right as the river takes a sharp bend to the right. Shortly afterwards, a bluff appears on river right, and a series of islands begins. The South Fork is simply gorgeous through these islands, which make for great places to have a shore lunch and to take pictures. The mountain scenery in the background adds to the appeal. After you pass by the islands, you will paddle for less than a half-mile before entering a river left bend; another island also comes into view. A granite hillside on river left further marks this area, and the smallmouth action can be quite fast. Riffles are numerous, and water willow beds occur from time to time. About a third of the trip has now been covered.

After the bend concludes, the South Fork becomes quite shallow for a while until more riffles come into view. The river left bank is part of the George Washington and Jefferson National Forest, so birdwatchers should be able to hear the lilting songs of a number of warblers and vireos. A powerline also crosses the river. A bluff then comes into view as the South Fork forms a river right curve, and Big Spring enters on river right. Expect to see cattle on river right and don't be surprised to see several of the bovines availing themselves of the refreshing water. The river then becomes very slow and deep for a quarter of a mile or so and the river forms a river left bend. Canoe camping is popular along this section as the national forest land continues. The Bealers Ferry canoe landing, which is classified as a primitive take-out and is accessible from Route 684, lies along the river left shore. At about the seven-mile point, yet another powerline crosses the South Fork, where the water is quite deep.

The last two miles of the Bixlers Bridge float offers superb smallmouth fishing. A river right bluff signals the beginning of that sport. Riffles, ledges, and water willow beds occur with great frequency. This area is known as Bumgardner's Falls, but only one Class I rapid is to be found and this one should be run right down the middle.

This is a great area for flyfishermen to employ nymphs and streamers, and spin fishermen should find success with just about any topwater lure. Foster's Landing on river left marks the end of a very delightful trip on the South Fork.

Note: Every year in late September, Christian Goebel and Shenandoah River Outfitters conduct a cleanup of the South Fork. Piles of trash are removed from the river and leave the stream a better place. This clean up campaign is an ideal way for civic groups and organizations such as the boy and girl scouts to be proactive. For more information, contact Shenandoah River Outfitters at the number listed in the appendix.

Angela Goebel checking out a deep-water ledge below Foster's Landing.

2.11
FOSTER'S TO BURNERS FORD

The Essentials

Trip: Foster's to Burners Ford, both in Page County. Refer to Map 5 in Appendix C.

USGS Quads: Rileyville and Bentonville

Distance: 9 miles

Rapids: Class II Compton Rapid, Class Is, and riffles

Access Points: At Foster's, a river left concrete ramp exists off Route 684 (Page Valley Road), which is now a gravel road. This ramp stops a foot above the streambed. Parking spaces are numerous in the gravel lot. **Note:** See "The Essentials" section of the preceding chapter for directions to the put-in.
At Burners Ford, the river right take-out is off Route 664 (Carvell Road) via Route 340. The take-out is a long, steep dirt ramp that is just downstream from a river right home on a high bank. Between the home and ramp is a concrete slab and wooden steps that lead up the bank. Parking is very limited.

Cara Sottosanti of Shenandoah River Outfitters told me a fascinating story concerning this section of the South Fork. During the Civil War, farmers who lived in the Burners Bottom area desperately tried to save their livestock from Union invaders, especially the troops of General Phillip Sheridan who had been ordered to destroy the crops and livestock in the Shenandoah Valley. The farmers finally came upon the idea to herd their cattle to a small, little-known cove called Fort Valley, which is across Massanutten Mountain. Fort Valley is so small that the Yankee troops were not aware of it, and the farmers succeeded in their gambit. The byway that they took to the secluded valley is today known as Lost Corner Road.

In August 1984, I first floated the South Fork of the Shenandoah, taking the Foster's Landing trip with Christian Goebel of Shenandoah River Outfitters. On that day, Christian and I had a memorable day of fishing, and I was entranced with the beauty of the river. If anything, my love for this river has grown as the years have gone by. This particular excursion remains one of my favorites on the South Fork as well as on any waterway. The Foster's Landing junket is a long day for anglers, and paddlers should allot a full half-day. Both groups should keep in mind that this is one of the most popular trips on the South Fork and that it receives heavy use, especially on weekends.

Much of that usage occurs around the Foster's Landing area, as wade fishing is popular there. A short paddle will take you away from the ramp and into a river left outside bend. Below the bend begins Goods Falls, a one-mile long section that offers outstanding angling. A powerline and scattered homes and trailers help mark this area, but the defining characteristic of Goods is that it is a wonderful place to paddle and fish. Only one Class I rapid (called, logically enough, the Goods Mill Rapid) exists in this section, but the ledges within create numerous riffles that paddlers will enjoy zipping through. These rock structures lend themselves to excellent hiding places for gamefish. On one float through this area with guide Capt'n Jack West, we talked to a couple that was fishing exclusively for redbreast sunfish. Together, they had caught approximately 50 of these panfish, all of them fooled by hellgrammites, and were planning a major fish fry the coming weekend. Jack and I tangled with some quality smallmouths, and we also saw an osprey that had enjoyed its own version of fishing success. Near the end of Goods Falls, you will come to Keysers Ford, a river-wide ledge across the South Fork.

After Goods Falls, the river becomes quite slow and shallow. The next point of note is Goods Landing, a river left take-out two miles into the float and off Page Valley Road. The ramp is concrete and parking spaces are numerous in the gravel lot. The Jefferson and George Washington National Forest lies along the river left bank, and this area is a popular place to camp. The South Fork then forms a river right curve. For the next nearly two miles, only scattered riffles dot the stream, and the fishing is only fair. The national forest continues along the river left bank. The South Fork then forms a river left bend and a large island comes into view. I have taken both passages around this island, but the right passageway is probably the better of the two. This arm of the South Fork then flows very straight once again with the occasional riffle and ledge offering fishing. Of note is the fact that another alternative take-out exists—the Seakford Landing on river left. The take-out is a concrete ramp and is off Page Valley Road; parking is limited.

On the aforementioned trip with Jack West, it was on this section that a rainstorm began and continued for much of the trip. I do not like fishing in a heavy rain. The constant falling of the raindrops, I believe, makes smallmouths cease to feed on the surface because they have difficulty picking out prey. Even if a hatch comes off at this time, the fish simply can not key in on it, making both fly and spin fishing difficult. Thus, my favorite tactic under these conditions is to strip a brightly colored weighted streamer or rapidly retrieve a deep running, orange or red crankbait. I want my offerings to be moving quickly and along the bottom, which is where I believe the bronzebacks are feeding. On the outing with West, I fooled a 16-inch smallmouth by using this tactic.

The South Fork then slows and deepens; muskie and channel catfish fans favor this part of the river. Several small bluffs line the river right shoreline and the river forms a river right bend at about the six-mile point. Soon you will hear, then see, Compton Rapids, a Class II. Christian Goebel once told me that he enjoys snorkeling below this rapid because of all the fishing gear he finds. Scout Compton's from the river right water willow bed that lies immediately above. You also may portage on that side. The dangerous part of Compton Rapids is a series of boulders that lie at the end and on the left. The best way to run this rapid is to start off down the center and then veer toward the right as you near its conclusion. In high water, some South Fork regulars rate this rapid as a Class III, making it the major rapid on the South Fork.

Immediately below Compton lies Golden Rocks on river right. This is a massive and very photogenic wall of Ordovician limestone that is a must-stop for photographers. The area is also a favorite of catfish anglers. The river then straightens once again and you will cover nearly two miles before coming to another river left bend. After you leave the bend, be prepared for some fun paddling and marvelous fishing. Burners Bottom lies on river left, and fields and scattered homes characterize this shoreline. Riffles and one Class I rapid occur during the last mile of this float, and the fishing action can be continuous. Some great bank cover, primarily sycamores and scattered rocks, exist and summertime anglers will likely score with topwater offerings. Be sure to watch for the Burners Ford river right take-out. It is nothing more than a steep dirt road that leads to the river. A river right home on a high bank comes right before the access point.

Christian Goebel supervises an annual September cleanup day on the South Fork of the Shenandoah.

2.12
BURNERS FORD TO BENTONVILLE

The Essentials

Trip: Burners Ford to Bentonville, in Page and Warren counties. Refer to Map 5 in Appendix C.

USGS Quad: Bentonville

Distance: 7 miles

Rapids: Class Is and riffles

Access Points: At Burners Ford, the river right put-in is off Route 664 (Carvell Road) via Route 340. The put-in is a long, steep dirt ramp that is just downstream from a river right home on a high bank. Between the home and ramp is a concrete slab and wooden steps that lead up the bank. Parking is very limited. At Bentonville, the river left take-out is off Route 613 (Indian Hollow Road) a few feet upstream from Indian Hollow Bridge, which is a low water bridge. The ramp is dirt, and parking spaces are available in the gravel ramp below the low water bridge.

Since 1984, Trace Noel has operated Shenandoah River Trips in Bentonville. He believes that one of the most fascinating aspects of the Shenandoah is the presence of Indian fish traps; that is, two piled rock walls that form a V closed at the downstream side. Native Americans made these dams so that fish could be herded into a confined area and then speared or trapped in wicker baskets. "When I am floating down the Shenandoah, I sometimes stop to think that the same stream I am canoeing was once navigated by Indians thousands of years ago," says Noel. "Some people believe that the fish dams were made during the Paleo-Indian period some 10,000 to 11,000 years ago. Others contend that the Woodland Indians made the dams much more recently. The Woodland Indians, also known as the Iroquois Nation, used the Shenandoah Valley as a place to fish and hunt. They also came to the valley, in particular Flint Run (which is a tributary of the Shenandoah), to gather flint. In fact, flint from Flint Run has been found as far west as Oklahoma."

Paddlers can negotiate the Burners Ford float in three or four hours, while float fishermen can hit the best spots in six or so hours. On the first half, this trip offers much better paddling, fishing, birdwatching, and scenery than on its second half. This is another South Fork excursion that remains one of my favorites. At the beginning, this float is very scenic. A rock garden and a series of ledges create superlative smallmouth habitat and make for marvelous photos as well. The hillside on river right keeps the river very shaded early in the morning, and the smallies often feed aggressively throughout that period. This area is further marked by a powerline that crosses the river. Guide Lou Kalina of Staunton raves about this section of the river, and Christian Goebel of Shenandoah River Outfitters rates it highly as well.

After you leave this section, you will come to a short river right bend where Overall Run enters on river right. A railroad bridge can also be seen from the hillside on river right. The river is very slow and deep in this area, known as the Overall Eddy, and continues for the next mile. The only exception is at the beginning where Leath's Ford exists. Kalina relates that Overall Eddy is a great wintertime fishing spot for big smallmouths, which tend to congregate in deep water that has numerous submerged ledges, as this eddy does.

At about the two-mile point, be prepared for some fun paddling and stupendous fishing. An old navigation dam creates an easy Class I rapid (run it center to right). This rapid is shortly followed by another Class I that has a boat sluice cut into it on the right side. The ledge has a two-foot drop. As you paddle downstream, note the river left bluffs that create marvelous photo opportunities and the fishing remains outstanding. Kalina prefers to use jig and pigs to probe the shoreline rock cover and the underwater ledges along the main channel. Next comes a riffle to Class I and a small island on river right, which are followed by the remains of a pair of wing dams. On one trip through here with Christian Goebel and his son Caleb, I watched the youngster catch several 6-to 8-inch long redbreast sunfish. The South Fork of the Shenandoah offers some of the best sport in Virginia for redbreasts, and they are a fun fish, especially for budding anglers. Friend Craig Fields insists that the Burners Ford float has the greatest concentration of citation sunfish (that is fish a pound or more) on the entire river.

At the three-mile point you'll approach the area known as Culler's Bottom, which continues for about a mile. National forest land exists on the river left bank, and canoe camping is possible. This area is also where Hazzard Mill operated during the 1800s. The fishing re-mains good as a number of ledges and small riffles dot the river. Next comes a small island, which is best run on its right side, and Broad Run enters on river right. At the four-mile point, three things mark the river: a powerline, a private river right ramp, and an island, which is best run on its right side. Then comes a riffle/Class I which was the location for Hazzard Mill dam. The rest of the trip offers very poor smallmouth fishing, but anglers should be able to catch all the sunfish they want. The river becomes fairly shallow and less scenic as a number of campers and homes lie along the river left bank. At about the five-mile point, the South Fork forms a river left bend, but the fishing does not improve. When you leave that bend, you will pass under a powerline, and spot pastures on both sides of the South Fork. This is a nice area to take pictures of the agrarian lifestyle that still so characterizes the Shenandoah Valley. A well-kept farm, with red barns, lies on river right and serves to remind that the Bentonville landing is close by. Be sure to take out above the low water bridge on river left. The bridge can be dangerous to run under when the river is at even moderate levels. At the bridge on river right, you will also spot two well-respected canoe liveries: Shenandoah River Trips and Downriver Canoe Company.

*Long rodders and other fishermen should relish the
Bentonville getaway.*

2.13
BENTONVILLE TO KARO

The Essentials

Trip: Bentonville to Karo, in Warren County. Refer to Map 6 in Appendix C.

USGS Quads: Bentonville and Strasburg

Distance: 8 miles

Rapids: Class Is and riffles

Access Points: At Bentonville, the river left put-in is off Route 613 (Indian Hollow Road) downstream from Indian Hollow Bridge, which is a low water bridge. The ramp is dirt, and parking spaces are available in the gravel ramp below the low water bridge. **Note:** Dirt ramps exist both above and below the bridge. At Karo, the river right take-out is at a gravel ramp on Gooney Run. At a river access sign, a gravel road (Chapman Farm Road) off Route 340 leads under a railroad bridge to the creek. To reach the access point, you will have to leave the South Fork, paddle through a slot in an islet, and cross Gooney Run. Parking is available in a gravel lot.

One of the most interesting aspects of the Shenandoah Valley's Civil War history is the continuing fascination that many Southerners have with General Stonewall Jackson. A must stop for those who admire the great leader is the Stonewall Jackson Museum at Hupp's Mill (540-465-5884) in Strasburg. Highlights of the museum include Civil War artifacts, reproductions of uniforms, weapons, and toys, and more than 100 photos of Jackson. For me, the most engaging thing about Jackson's military prowess is how he and his seventeen thousand men defeated sixty thousand Union soldiers in a series of battles during the Shenandoah Valley Campaign of 1862. Remarkably, Jackson's tactics from that campaign are still studied in military schools today.

The Bentonville getaway is four-to-five hours for paddlers and seven or eight-hours for float fishermen. Birdwatchers will find this trip very rewarding as the shoreline habitat is populated by species such as yellow warblers, Louisiana waterthrush, and orchard orioles. For the first mile or so, fields and pastures characterize both shorelines, and a few riffles dot the streambed. A river left outside bend, replete with sycamores, also comes in this first mile; Route 613 follows the curve of the stream. The good fishing begins near the beginning of the second mile as a series of riffles and ledges occur; some of these ledges have the potential to become Class Is in high water. Once on a float through this section of the Bentonville trip with guide Lou Kalina, I noted him using some of the baits made by two well-known Virginia lure makers, Charlie Case of Clarksville and Butch Neal of Saltville. The former is known for his realistic hellgrammite and mad tom creations and the latter for his handcrafted jigs. I have always found it gratifying that local fisher-men are often loyal to state lure makers, which, of course, is commend-able. On this particular trip, I caught bass that fell for the Case Hellgrammite while Kalina scored with Neal's jigs.

A fish dam comes after those riffles and itself creates a riffle. A powerline then crosses the South Fork and the river makes a river right bend at the two-mile point. Be prepared for some excellent fishing and fun paddling as for nearly a mile, ledges and riffles occur non-stop. A flyfishermen entering this section during the afternoon should find damsel and dragonfly hatches to match, and spinfishermen will likely find the topwater action to be continuous. An Indian fish dam marks the end of this section; run this riffle/Class I on far river left. Next you will note a creek entering on river right and a gravel ramp; you have reached the Raymond R. (Andy) Guest State Park. Excellent ledge and riffle-type cover now exists for more than a half mile, and individuals entering the river from the park will find pleasant wade fishing. Two more state park ramps lie along the river right shoreline in this section. I enjoy tossing 6-inch plastic worms and weighted crayfish patterns in this type of habitat. The river then forms a river right curve, with ledges and riffles interspersed, and then for another mile riffles characterize the float. Cows feed along both shorelines, and the fishing remains good.

After the South Fork forms a river left bend, you will come to a section known as The Point. The Point occurs at the five-mile-mark of this float and continues for more than a mile. Quite logically, The Point begins as a projection on river left, and homes lie all along this projection. McCoy's Falls also characterizes the river through here. Once again on the South Fork, the word *falls* does not mean rapids as these falls are nothing more than riffle after riffle which can metamorphose into Class I rapids only during high water. These riffles also provide plenty of places for brown bass to hide. At the end of McCoy's Falls, you will see a very shallow ledge spanning the river and two islands directly below it. This is McCoy's Ford and is where some of Stonewall Jackson's troops traversed the South Fork in the spring of 1862. According to *The Shenandoah River Atlas*, the Southerners were on their way to sever communications between Strasburg and Front Royal as a prelude to a Yankee attack.

After another long series of riffles, you will soon pass under two more power lines; only a mile is left in the Bentonville float. On one float through this section I once spotted a Louisiana waterthrush feeding along the shore, bobbing up and down in its characteristic manner. Without a doubt, the three loud, lilting notes at the beginning of this bird's song, which are followed by a jumbled, descending warble, are one of the most welcome sounds on any river. I relish listening to this avian whether I am on a mountain rill or a valley river like the South Fork. Next, you will come to another series of riffles/Class Is, which have deep-water ledges that offer good fishing. Some bluffs then appear on river right as do more riffles and an easy Class I. Flint Run enters on river right and a large deep pool forms—within the pool are numerous ledges and rocks. Soon the Karo access point, with its gravel parking lot, will be spotted on river right. The first mile upstream from Karo is a popular destination for boats powered by electric trolling motors.

Karo to Front Royal is one of the premier trips on the South Fork.

2.14
KARO TO FRONT ROYAL

The Essentials

Trip: Karo to Front Royal, both in Warren County. Refer to Map 6 in
  Appendix C.

USGS Quads: Bentonville, Strasburg, and Front Royal

Distance: 6 miles

Rapids: A Class II, Class Is, and riffles

Access Points: At Karo, the river right put-in is at a gravel ramp on
  Gooney Run. At a river access sign, a gravel road (Chapman
  Farm Road) off Route 340 leads under a railroad bridge to the
  creek. You will have to paddle across Gooney Run and through
  a slot in an islet to reach the South Fork. Parking is available in
  a gravel lot. At Front Royal, the river right take-out is at a
  concrete ramp a few feet downstream from a concrete dock.
  Route 681 (Criser Road) via Route 340 leads to the ramp.
  Parking spaces are numerous in the gravel lot.

Less than a 30-minute drive from Front Royal lies the charming village of Washington in Rappahannock County. This community, numbering only a few hundred people, was the first town to be named for George Washington. Interestingly, the town has never outgrown the five block by two block grid that Washington laid out when he surveyed the area in the mid-1700s. Just outside of Washington, often called Little Washington by locals, is one of Elaine's and my favorite B&Bs, the Caledonia Farm-1812. Owner Phil Irwin's B&B has the Shenandoah National Park as its backdrop, and Irwin had donated an easement on the property to the Virginia Outdoors Foundation. That means the property will always retain its rural status (see chapter on the Caledonia Farm and the Virginia Outdoors Foundation).

The Karo float is one of my favorites on the South Fork, and a trip that I try to take every time that I am in the Front Royal area. Paddlers can easily complete this jaunt in several hours, and float fishermen will find it doable in six hours or so. The most intense whitewater on this float occurs at the very beginning as a Class II called Karo Rapid. Actually, Karo is not always a Class II, as it dwindles to a rolling Class I in the low water of summer. Boulders line the river left side, but a fairly wide chute leads down the heart of the rapid and is easy to locate. Karo lies to the left of a bar, and you can avoid this rapid altogether by floating or dragging your craft down the right side of the islet. If you are without a boat, the area downstream from the put-in is a popular place to wet wade for smallmouths, rock bass, and redbreast sunfish.

After you fish and/or paddle through the rock-laden pool below Karo Rapid, note that the river begins a lazy two-mile bend to the left. The first half mile or so features especially slow water and one very ominous sign on river left: "Warning: Deliverance Starts Here. No trespassing." I do not recommend stopping at this landmark for a shorelunch. The river right shoreline is heavily wooded while the left bank is a mixture of homes and fields. One species of songbird that is abundant on this float is the Eastern kingbird. I rarely encounter kingbirds on the James or New rivers, but on the South Fork, this bird is very visible. Expect to frequently hear its "kit-kit-kitter" note. Also don't be surprised to spot plenty of great blue and green herons along this section. I once saw five great blue herons in one area of this float, possibly an adult pair along with its nearly grown offspring.

The first major feature below Karo Rapid is an island about a mile into the float. You can scoot down either side of the island, but the right side probably offers the best fishing. Below the island lies a river-wide ledge as well as more ledges and riffles. Once while Elaine and I were floating this section, I hooked what surely must have been a 4-pound bass on a popper. The fish struck the popper as soon as it landed under a sycamore. The brute then charged toward deep water and our canoe, leaping at the boat and throwing the popper. Flyfishermen will want to try surface offerings through here while spinfishermen will likely score with buzzbaits, Rebel Pop Rs, Heddon Tiny Torpedos, Rapala Skitter Pop and Props, and Berkley Frenzy Poppers.

About halfway through the bend, you will come across another island; the best pathway is on the left side while the best fishing is frequently on the heavily shaded right passageway. I have caught some nice smallies both above and below this island. A series of ledges and gentle riffles dot the river below the island and provide more solid sport. You will float by one more island on this bend, and the river continues to flow at a good clip. Soon you will come to a point on river right and you will see water willow, sycamores, and a campground on river right. This area marks the beginning of Kings Eddy, which extends for more than a half mile. Some river right bluffs add beauty to the eddy, and fields and a silo distinguish the left shoreline; but this area offers poor angling for smallmouths. The Front Royal Canoe Company also has a private take-out through a culvert on river right. The livery lies on a hill above the South Fork.

After Kings Eddy terminates, prepare for some fabulous fishing for more than two miles as the South Fork makes another horseshoe bend to the right. Ledges, riffles, and water willow covered islets characterize most of this section. Occasional homes and docks line the river left shoreline while sycamores, silver maples, and box elders flourish along both banks. Several deep runs exist along the river left shoreline and are excellent places to prospect for mossybacks. Toward the second half of the bend, you will encounter a river wide ledge that forms a riffle and that may be the remains of a dam. Shortly afterwards, you will see a natural ledge that extends from the river right shoreline and, below that, more underwater ledges and numerous riffles. An avid angler can easily spend three hours in this bend and the summertime action for both the long rodder and spinfisherman can be phenomenal. Generally, I like to employ four rods on any given trip: a medium heavy baitcaster (for soft plastic baits), a medium heavy spinning rod (for jig and pigs and spinnerbaits) and a medium spinning rod (for topwater lures). The last member of the quartet is a fly rod (ideal for surface patterns, Clouser minnows, and streamers). All four of these rods should receive a proper workout on this section.

After the bend concludes, the next major feature is the Blakemore's Mill Dam ruins, which form a Class I rapid. (This rapid is sometimes called Three Chute Rapid.) Take the middle pathway for easiest navigation, and be sure to work the eddies below the water willow beds immediately downstream. A powerline then spans the South Fork, and dozens of small boulders litter the river right shoreline. Route 340 runs along much of this bank. After you pass the last of these boulders, you will have to paddle for some ten minutes through very deep, slow moving water. The river is very silted, and angling opportunities are limited. A white building on a ridge helps mark the river right take-out as do a white buoy and a concrete pier. As my wife and I have discovered on several occasions, the Karo float is a fine getaway for couples.

Elaine Ingram paddling the Front Royal to Riverton section

2.15
FRONT ROYAL TO RIVERTON

The Essentials
Trip: Front Royal to Riverton, both in Warren County. Refer to Map 6 in Appendix C.

USGS Quads: Front Royal

Distance: 4 miles

Rapids: Class I/Riffles

Access Points: At Front Royal, the river right put-in is at a concrete ramp a few feet downstream from a concrete dock. Route 681 (Criser Road) via Route 340 leads to the ramp. Parking spaces are numerous in the gravel lot. At Riverton, the river left take-out is a concrete ramp on the North Fork of the Shenandoah. The ramp is off Route 637 (Guard Hill Road) via Route 340. Parking spaces are numerous in the gravel lot. To reach the take-out, paddlers will have to come to the confluence of the North and South Forks and then paddle upstream on the North Fork for several hundred yards. The access point is directly below a dam.

Sometimes, American history is not about what is good and true but what has become a legacy of shame. Sadly, the latter case exists twice on the Shenandoah system. Today, various contaminant and advisory/restrictions exist on the South River, the South Fork of the Shenandoah, and the Main Stem because of mercury releases decades ago from the Dupont plant in Waynesboro, which lies on the South River. In July of 2002 while doing research for this book, I encountered Virginia Department of Game and Inland Fisheries biologist Steve Reeser who was taking mercury samples from fish that had been shocked near the Front Royal ramp. Amazingly, years after Dupont committed its acts, the mercury levels in fish have not decreased says Reeser. Those mercury levels are the reason why the Virginia Department of Health Restrictions and Health Advisories has decreed that from the South River "fish caught should not be consumed" and from the South Fork that people should "eat no more than two 8-ounce meals per month of fish caught from these waters. Small children, nursing mothers, pregnant women, and women who may become pregnant should not eat fish from these waters."

The other infamous case involves the old Avtex Fibers (also known as Viscose) plant in Front Royal. Because of PCB's once released from that plant, "fish caught should not be consumed" from the Route 619 Bridge near Front Royal downstream on the South Fork and Main Stem to the West Virginia state line. Incredibly, in 1987, Avtex Fibers released 54,173,150 pounds of highly hazardous toxic chemicals, making it Virginia's worst polluting industry and the twenty-sixth worst in the country. Joe Trento, head of the Natural Resources News Service, told me about the history of the old Viscose plant. Trento said that the need for the plant was based upon a request from President Franklin Roosevelt and Prime Minister Winston Churchill during World War II to have rayon insulation for tanks. By the end of the war, massive fish kills had begun on the South Fork and Main Stem. The U.S. Government, said Trento, continued to cover up what it was doing, going so far as to have a government official, during the first President Bush administration, secretly state before a closed session of Congress that the government "had to keep the plant open for national security reasons, when, in fact, it didn't." Virginia state attorney general Mary Sue Terry finally ordered Avtex shut down in 1990. "Virginia," says Trento, "has one of the most deplorable environmental records of any state in the Union." Trento concludes that when he first came to the area he was horrified by the amount of pollution that Avtex was belching into Virginia's air and water. He was told by one local person that the stench coming from the plant "smells like jobs." Trento's retort was that the stench "smells like cancer to me." Not surprisingly, when Avtex closed, Front Royal's economy improved as the city's natural attractiveness was showcased, and reputable businesses wanted to open. Once more proving that what is good for the environment is often good for the economy of a locale, a point that many politicians (their pockets stuffed with campaign donations from polluting industries) refuse to understand or can not understand.

Don Roberts, who operates the Front Royal Canoe Company, says that fishermen and paddlers rarely ask to float from the Front Royal landing to Riverton, because of the negative history of the area. However, Roberts notes that the smallmouth bass population has rebounded on the section and that local people are catching great numbers of fish from the river. Paddlers can easily negotiate the Front Royal float in two hours, and fishermen will need no more than four hours. At the put-in, you will see a gauging station and old wood barn on river left. Soon you will float under a powerline and spot a large concrete building, which was a pumping station, on river right. Through the first two miles or so, the entire river right shoreline was the property of the Avtex Fibers plant. These two miles are remarkably consistent in their makeup. The river flows very gently with occasional small riffles, and smallmouth bass and sunfish fin about in the rock-lined pools. Near the end of the two miles, you will see a concrete wall on river right.

The South Fork then makes a river left bend, and for the next half-mile, some above average angling opportunities exist as a very long riffle ensues. Punches Run enters on river left and a powerline crosses the river, marking the beginning of that fishing. Kendrick's Ford, a very shallow section, bisects the riffle. Sycamores line both banks, and the community of Riverton can be seen on river left. At the end of the riffle, solid deep-water sport exists, as large rocks line the bottom and a fair current sends you along. The Route 340/522 Bridge also crosses. By the time you come to three small islands that lie in a line across the river, the good fishing is over. Paddle quickly under two railroad bridges and make a left turn when the North Fork of the Shenandoah commingles with the South Fork to form the Shenandoah. Then paddle upstream for about 15 minutes until you reach the river left put-in, located below a low water dam. Both banks of the North Fork show the signs of civilization; campers especially dot the river right shoreline. Fortunately, the North Fork flows very gently so the paddle upstream is not a problem. Interestingly, the Front Royal float gives you the opportunity to paddle in three rivers on the same trip, although, technically, you are only in the Main Stem for a few seconds.

Part Three
*Main Stem of the Shenandoah
in Virginia and West Virginia*

Craig Fields paddling down the North Fork where it and the South Fork commingle to form the Main Stem.

3.1
RIVERTON TO MORGAN'S FORD

The Essentials

Trip: Riverton to Morgan's Ford, both in Warren County. Refer to Map 7 in Appendix C.

USGS Quads: Front Royal and Linden

Distance: 6½ miles

Rapids: Class Is/Riffles

Access Points: At Riverton, the river left put-in is a concrete ramp on the North Fork of the Shenandoah. The ramp is off Route 637 (Guard Hill Road) via Route 340. Parking spaces are numerous in the gravel lot. At Morgan's Ford, the river right take-out is at a gravel ramp immediately above the Route 624 (Milldale Road) low water bridge, which is reached via Route 661 (Fairground Road) and Route 522. Canoe passage under the bridge is impossible. Parking spaces are numerous in the gravel lot.

The previous chapter's historical anecdote dealt with some historical infamy regarding pollution in the Front Royal area. But today, there are many reasons to visit this charming town; in fact, Front Royal is one of the favorite places for my wife Elaine and me to visit. Bob Pickrell, who along with Don LeFever mans the Front Royal-Warren County Visitor's Center, likes to regale visitors with the history of the area.

"Front Royal developed into a crossroads town when settlers came to the Shenandoah Valley during the 1700s," says Pickrell. "The community was called Lehew Town, named by French Huguenots who were early settlers. In 1788, the town was chartered as Front Royal, which received its name during a Revolutionary War training exercise. A drill instructor told the troops to 'front the royal oak' that was standing, and the town received its name from that command."

The War Between the States brought great turmoil to Front Royal, and Civil War enthusiasts will relish a visit to the community. The town has at least sixteen different Civil War historical sites, but my favorite involves the story of Mosby's Rangers. In brief, Mosby's Rangers, led by Confederate John S. Mosby, conducted a series of guerilla raids against the Yankee forces of General Phillip Sheridan. Mosby's hit and run tactics infuriated Sheridan, so much so that when six Rangers were captured in battle, he ordered them executed. The officer carrying out the execution was General George Custer, who history, unfortunately, would hear from again.

I have only taken the Riverton trip one time, and that was with friend Craig Fields of Dumfries. Nearing the end of this float, I asked Craig if he would ever undergo it again, and he pointedly said no. I agreed. The reason for Craig's and my disgust with this excursion is the 3½-mile stretch of slow water that begins the Riverton junket, and a several hundred yard long portage around the Warren Hydropower Dam that must be endured. With the portage, paddlers must allot four hours for this trip and float fishermen may need as many as seven hours.

The Riverton trip begins with a fifteen minute paddle down the North Fork of the Shenandoah (see the preceding chapter) until you reach the Main Stem of the Shenandoah. A railroad bridge crosses the Main Stem, and the water is quite deep. A conveyor belt then extends across the river, and the river right bank is very wooded while scattered fields characterize the left shoreline. Throughout this area, and the entire stretch behind the dam, the Shenandoah is very slow and deep. Catfish and carp fans will find this water to their liking, while anglers interested in largemouth bass will find success around the many downed trees. Smallmouth bass fishermen will likely be extremely disappointed. The next focal point is the Interstate 66 Bridge that crosses the river; you have now paddled about two miles from the put-in. As you continue downstream, you will spot a private ramp and a bluff on river right and a country club on river left. Both shorelines to the dam are quite unremarkable. Scattered woods, a river left bluff, and omnipresent powerboats during the warm weather season are about all that is worth noting. The dam is easily seen as are the red buoys that stretch across the river and two warning signs that mark the river left portage. The good part about the portage is that the terrain is very flat, and a gravel path makes the going relatively easy. The long distance exhausted both Craig and me. Another point of interest is that the ramps above and below the dam are made of cinderblocks. The ramp below the portage lies at the bottom of a short, steep hill.

Earlier, I wrote that I would not take the entire Riverton float again, which is true, but the fishing below the dam to the take-out can be quite good. Access to the river can be gained via Route 620, which runs near the portage path. Wade fishermen especially will find the walk to the river very doable, but float fishermen will find the boat carry arduous. If access were easier, I would love float fishing the stretch below the dam. Riffles and water willow beds lie immediately below the dam as do a series of deep-water ledges. This type of habitat continues, with the periodic riffle, until you come to a river left outside curve, known as Horseshoe Bend. Is there any river in the two Virginias that does not have at least one section known as "Horseshoe Bend?" All of this section offers smallmouth bass potential.

Then you come to Cowtail Rapids, also known as Berkleys Falls. This is a half mile or so section of riffles that can occasionally metamorphose into a Class I rapid or two. Island Ford lies near the end of Cowtail Rapids. This section is where you should allot most of your fishing time, as Fields and I did quite well here. The rest of the float consists mostly of scattered rocky pools. Both wade fishermen and canoers make their way upstream from the Morgan's Ford access point, which is easily spotted from well upstream.

The Morgan's Ford float is a favorite of guide Alec Burnett, shown here.

3.2
MORGAN'S FORD TO BERRY'S FERRY

The Essentials

Trip: Morgan's Ford in Warren County to Berry's Ferry in Clarke County. Refer to Map 7 in Appendix C.

USGS Quads: Linden, Boyce, and Ashby Gap

Distance: 11 miles

Rapids: Class IIs, Is, and riffles

Access Points: At Morgan's Ford, the river right put-in is at a gravel ramp immediately below the Route 624 (Milldale Road) low water bridge, which is reached via Route 661 (Fairground Road) and Route 522. Canoe passage under the bridge is impossible. Parking spaces are numerous in the gravel lot. At Berry's Ferry, the river left take-out is a concrete ramp under the Route 50 Bridge (Byrd Bridge). Route 622 (Swift Shoals Road) leads to the take-out via Route 50. Parking is available in the gravel lot under the bridge.

111

A landmark on the Morgan's Ferry excursion is Robinson Crusoe Island, which brings to mind the literary classic of the same name. Literary historians say that eighteenth century Americans had three books in their homes: the Bible, *Pilgrim's Progress*, and *Robinson Crusoe*. The Bible remains a best seller today, but today's Americans generally have not heard of *Pilgrim's Progress*, and *Robinson Crusoe* is nothing more than a character in a condensed children's book to many young people. The original *Robinson Crusoe*, written by Daniel Defoe, is a classic British novel about a man's struggle to survive on a deserted Caribbean island. I recently reread this tome and the adventure story that Defoe penned in 1719 was just as engrossing as when I first read it in college. So much so that I assigned the novel to my tenth graders to read (I am a high school English teacher). By their naming of an island after Defoe's main character, the early residents of the Shenandoah Valley were also apparently quite familiar with this classic work.

The Morgan's Ford excursion is a long afternoon trip for paddlers and a full day journey for float fishermen. I have seen bald eagles and ospreys on this float, and bird watchers will find the viewing for warblers, vireos, waterfowl, and shorebirds quite satisfactory. I first took this float with guide Alec Burnett, who operates Shenandoah Lodge in Luray. Burnett rates the Morgan's Ford junket best of the four possible trips on the Main Stem in the Old Dominion. Rain began to fall as we launched and for the next four hours continued, sometimes quite heavily. The bass fishing was poor throughout. I believe that moderate to heavy rainfall causes smallmouths to stop foraging. I feel this is so because the constant pattering of raindrops on the surface disorients the fish and makes their senses function less effectively, thus making them unable to detect food sources easily, especially surface prey. If you are faced with fishing during the rain, consider using sound making lures such as crankbaits. During the rainy day trip with Burnett, for example, I was able to entice several nice bass with a Bandit 200 series crankbait and a Big O. Spinnerbaits are another prudent choice under these conditions.

After you launch at Morgan's Ford, you will cruise through some gentle, shallow riffles and then pass by farmland for the first-mile-plus of the trip. Sycamores line both banks, but the water is fairly shallow and bass holding areas along the shoreline are scarce. Some fair mid-river habitat exists in the form of submerged boulders. At about 1¼ miles, you will spot an island; take the right channel for the best path. For nearly the next mile or so, scattered boulders and mid-river shelves characterize the stream bottom. Howellsville Branch enters on river right at about the 2¼-mile marker. As we neared the branch, Burnett told me that he often glimpses bald eagles in this area; and as if on cue, one of these majestic raptors appeared shortly afterwards. One of the major conservation successes of the past 30 years has been the restoration of the bald eagle to much of its historic range. Watching this predator fish on my initial Morgan's Ford trip was a thrill.

After Howellsville Branch enters, fishing opportunities abound for the next two miles. An island soon appears (take the right passage) and riffles form at its end, offering an excellent opportunity for flyfishermen to toss streamers and nymphs. For spin fishermen, I recommend casting buzzbaits and grubs. On river left, sycamores (which form canopies over deeper water) create bass habitat, as do deep-water ledges, water willow beds, and more riffles. A mile after Howellsville Branch (and three-plus-miles from the float's beginning), Ashby's Falls looms—a Class II rapid. The only path is on far river left where a boat sluice was cut through the two-foot-ledge. Burnett rates the smallmouth angling both above and below Ashby's as outstanding; a ledge-filled pool exists below the falls. Bank to bank ledges also lie below this pool; a white house on river left helps mark this area, as does Saw Mill Creek, which enters on river left.

The next major feature is a Class I-II rapid, which has had a boat sluice created on far river right. This sluice offers the best passageway in terms of water flow, but some overhanging trees may cause problems. Fields and sycamores along both shorelines characterize the next half-mile as riffles send you on your way. When Dry Run enters on river right, you have reached the 4½-mile point of the float. Over the next mile, bass fishing opportunities are limited, as the river is quite shallow and straight with only a few scattered ledges. A riffle then forms at the head of Treasure Island, signaling some fetching fishing. Take the left passageway around the island for the best route and smallmouth sport. *Note:* Don't confuse Treasure Island with the islet that lies to its left.

Near the end of Treasure Island, Hardin's Island begins and continues for well over a mile. Riffles and water willow beds mark the beginning of Hardin's Island; the only path is around its left side. Dropoffs and midstream boulders characterize the stream bottom and make for great places to work weighted streamers and soft plastic baits. High banks also characterize this section, giving the floater the impression that he is far from civilization. I once caught a channel catfish on the Morgan's Ford float, a fact not unusual except that the cat mauled a crankbait. About once every 10 years or so while fishing a river, I experience this oddball happening. Other anglers also report this happening from time to time; who knows what conditions cause channel catfish to suddenly take a liking to fast moving lures.

At the end of Hardin's Island, enticing streamside rock cover is visible both above and below the surface. You have now covered about seven miles of the float. The next major feature is Lover's Leap, a rock bluff on river left. Lovers today would have to take a long flight off this bluff if they would like to reach deep water. Could it be that the water level of the Main Stem has changed greatly over the years, or is it possible that lovers did more talking than leaping in earlier times? In any event, the riffles and deep-water ledges below Lover's Leap offer excellent fishing, as do the scattered ledges over the next mile of the excursion. At about the nine-mile point, you will note a private concrete ramp on river right; do not trespass.

The final two miles can be easily summarized. This section begins with the Class I-II Swift Shoals rapid. The best passageways exist in the middle of Swift Shoals. Water willow beds characterize this area and provide more good fishing. This rapid exists because of the remains of Swift Shoals Mill, which was in operation during the 1800s. Route 638 follows the river right bank, providing access for wade fishermen. After you pass Swift Shoals, you will float through some fairly slow moving water. You will also pass by Robinson Crusoe Island; take the left route. A half-mile or so of paddling will bring you to the Route 50 Bridge and the river left take-out under it.

Alec Burnett, shown here, feels that The Main Stem offers big small-mouth potential. This bass that he caught on the Berry's Ferry float proves it.

3.3
BERRY'S FERRY TO LOCKES

The Essentials

Trip: Berry's Ferry to Lockes, both in Clarke County. Refer to Map 8 in Appendix C.

USGS Quads: Boyce and Ashby Gap

Distance: 10 miles

Rapids: One Class II, Class Is and riffles

Access Points: At Berry's Ferry, the river left put-in is a concrete ramp under the Route 50 Bridge (Byrd Bridge). Route 622 (Swift Shoals Road) leads to the take-out via Route 50. Parking is available in the gravel lot under the bridge. At Lockes, the river left take-out is a concrete ramp off Route 621 (Martin Road) via Route 255, Route 617 (Stubblefield Road) and Route 340. Parking is available in a gravel lot.

Every war is filled with minor players that in their own way influenced history. Such is the case with Confederate spy Belle Boyd. Bob Pickrell, manager of the Front Royal-Warren County Visitors Center, calls Boyd "the Mata Hari of the Civil War." Before the Battle of Front Royal in May 1862, Boyd was visiting her aunt at the Strickler Hotel. Boyd hid in a cottage behind the hotel and overheard Union Colonel John Kenly discussing battle strategy. She slipped out of the cottage, through enemy lines, and informed General Stonewall Jackson of the Yankee's plans. On May 23, aided by Boyd's information, Jackson defeated Kenly and captured six hundred of his soldiers. The Belle Boyd Cottage can be visited on Chester Street in Front Royal today.

Quite simply, the Berry's Ferry float is one of the best on the entire Shenandoah system. The shoreline has few homes and is almost entirely wooded, seeing bald eagles is a possibility, the birding is extraordinary, and the fishing and canoeing rate as excellent. Paddlers will need a full half-day to drift through this section while float fishermen will need an entire day to work all the areas. Upon launching, you will soon come to an island; either passage offers plenty of water. If you paddle to the left of the island, do not go to the right of the next land mass, which is Burwell Island. Burwell is one of the longest islands in Virginia, and the right passageway is very narrow and shallow.

Burwell extends for about a mile and three quarters and is heavily wooded. During the spring especially, hark to the sounds of birds that thrive in riparian zones such as spotted sandpipers, hooded warblers, and orchard orioles. Scattered rocks and boulders lie along the streambed, and a good mixture of deep water and shallow runs exists. At the tip of Burwell lies Long Island and it too must be negotiated on its left side. I first took the Berry's Ferry excursion with guide Alec Burnett who operates Shenandoah Lodge in Luray. While we were drifting by Long Island, Burnett regaled me with tales of monster carp, fish 10 pounds and larger, that he had caught by drifting nymphs with his flyrod. While I was openly doubting his tales of jousting with jumbo carp by nymphing, I caught a fair size carp that hit my crankbait. Anything is possible in the fishing realm. Smallmouth bass are the more likely quarry along Long Island as riffles and a rocky substrate predominate.

At about the three-mile point, you will float over a ledge, pass under a powerline, and then drift over another rock ledge. This entire area proffers excellent angling and picture taking. Sluices appear to have been cut through the ledges, and the smallies stack-up above and below the drops in the stream bottom. Next you will enter a river left outside bend; this is the Calmes Neck area. Route 621 runs along part of the river left bank, providing access for wade fishermen. This is also the area that is known for its eagle sightings as the shoreline is heavily wooded and many snags exist for these birds of prey to perch. When Shan Hill Branch dribbles in on river left at the four-mile point, be prepared for some fun paddling and stupendous smallmouth sport. For nearly a mile, you will course through riffles and two Class Is, both of which offer plenty of passages. Burnett, who is an expert with both fly and spinning gear, likes to toss what he calls "meat fly patterns" in this type of riffle/ledge habitat. Meat flies, by the guide's definition, are 5-inch (or longer) streamers that salt water sportsmen often employ for bonefish. Burnett, though, has enjoyed great success with overgrown smallies that smack these streamers. On our trip, for example, I watched as two very fine bronzebacks simultaneously converged on one of his meat flies. I also saw him land a 22-inch smallmouth that fell for a twin-tail grub. Few anglers are as adept with flies and lures as Burnett.

At about the half way point of the Berry's Ferry junket, you will come to two more ledges that appear to have had sluices cut through them. You will enter a river right curve. The second half of this curve features very thin water and an island; paddle around it on the right. Then ensue a number of riffles and ledges and the only Class II on this getaway; run this rapid on its far left. It is being redundant to say that more excellent fishing exists in this area; the bass habitat is almost non-stop on this 10-miler, which is just as much fun to float as it is to fish. At about the nine-mile point, you will enter into a river left curve, and Route 621 once more comes down along the Main Stem. Coming out of the bend, you will spot some houses along the river left shoreline, a powerline, and Craig Run entering the Main Stem. Next up is Lockes Landing on river left.

The Lockes to Castleman's Ferry trip provides good fishing and paddling.

3.4
LOCKES TO CASTLEMAN'S FERRY

The Essentials

Trip: Lockes to Castleman's Ferry, both in Clarke County. Refer to Map 8 in Appendix C.

USGS Quads: Boyce and Ashby Gap

Distance: 5 miles

Rapids: Class Is and riffles

Access Points: At Lockes, the river left take-out is a concrete ramp off Route 621 (Martin Road) via Route 255, Route 617 (Stubblefield Road) and Route 340. Parking is available in a gravel lot. At Castleman's Ferry, the take-out is at the river right Route 7 Bridge (via Route 340). Parking is available in the gravel lot under the bridge.

Since this entire section of river flows through Clarke County, I find it appropriate to delve briefly into the life history of the county's namesake, Revolutionary War hero George Rogers Clark. Born in Charlottesville, Virginia, Clark played a crucial role in the battle with the British over the Northeast Territory. In 1778 and 1779, Clark, commanding some 175 men, defeated the superior (in numbers that is) British forces in three separate battles. In 1783, Thomas Jefferson offered Clark the chance to explore west of the Mississippi River. Clark rejected the offer, but, ironically, 20 years later, Jefferson tabbed Clark's younger brother William to conduct the same exploration with Meriwether Lewis. Perhaps you have heard of the Lewis and Clark Expedition.

Paddlers can easily undergo the Lockes getaway in three hours or so, and float fishermen will only need a half-day to practice their sport. I confess that Alec Burnett and I once float fished the 22 miles from Berry's Ferry in Virginia to Avon Bend (also known as Meyer's Ferry) in West Virginia in 12 hours. Alec did yeoman work that day, oaring his raft the entire distance and was exhausted at the end of the trip, as was I. We both knew that taking on such a long trip in mid-July was foolhardy, but we underwent it anyway. I once read that males have a tendency to want to conquer things; for example, when I was a child, my dad always refused to stop when we were going somewhere. From the backseat of the Ford, I would complain mightily; however, as an adult, I have the same compulsion to "conquer the road" or "conquer the river" that my dad did. My dubious personal record for most river miles paddled in a day is 32, an outpouring of energy that left me feeling like a dead man for several days.

Houses and other man-made structures are common along the Lockes float, and many of them line the river left bank in the first mile. The first landmark is in this initial mile as Grigsby's Island (also known as Shepherd's Island) cleaves the river. The left passageway offers the best paddling and fishing; I once caught a 3-pound-plus smallie there that fell for a topwater offering. At the end of Grigsby's Island, look for the remains of a milldam that create a riffle. The shallow area below the remains is known as Shepherd's Ford and Ferry. For the next mile or so, Watermelon Park dominates the river left shoreline. This is a campground for tubers and campers, so expect to see many people using this portion of the Main Stem on weekends.

A series of riffles then dot the streambed, offering fair to good smallmouth and redbreast sunfish action. A powerline also crosses the river and Morgan's Island is reached; you have now covered two miles of the Lockes float. Take the right passageway around Morgan's Island and after passing the island, course through a series of riffles. Morgan's Ford lies part way through this riffle zone. Again, the fishing is satisfactory although certainly not great, and the scenery could be rated much the same. More homes and campers line both shorelines. After the riffles terminate, the Shenandoah alternates periodically between deep, rocky pools and shallow runs. At the three-mile point, Scheel Branch enters on river right, and Route 606 can be seen on the same side a short distance downstream.

The next mile or so offers some enticing and sporadic bank fishing, especially on river right. River birches, silver maples, and sycamores line that shore, and evening floats can find the bass feeding on the surface. The next landmark is where Joe Bell's Branch enters on river right, which is identified by an arch bridge over the creek. Take the right route by a cluster of islets and you will shortly arrive at the river right take-out at Castleman's Ferry, the last access point in the Old Dominion.

The Castleman's Ferry to Avon Bend float begins in Virginia but ends in West Virginia.

3.5
CASTLEMAN'S FERRY (VIRGINIA) TO AVON BEND, ALSO KNOWN AS MEYER'S FERRY (WEST VIRGINIA)

The Essentials

Trip: Castleman's Ferry in Clarke County to Avon Bend, also known as Meyer's Ferry, in Jefferson County, West Virginia. Refer to Map 8 in Appendix C.

USGS Quads: Ashby Gap, Berryville, and Round Hill

Distance: 7 miles

Rapids: A Class I and riffles

Access Points: At Castleman's Ferry, the put-in is a concrete ramp on river right below the Route 7 Bridge (via Route 340). Parking is available in the gravel lot under the bridge. At Avon Bend, the river left take-out is a gravel/dirt slide that is nothing more than an opening in the shoreline. **Note:** The roads leading to the take-out are poorly marked and do not have route numbers listed on signs. The signs themselves are hand-lettered. From Route 340, take Smith Road, Ward Clipp Road, Kabletown Road, and Dutch Hill Road to the access point. Most of these roads are gravel. Parking is very limited at the take-out.

123

Jefferson County is named for the third president, Thomas Jefferson, a founding father, author of the Declaration of Independence, and founder of the University of Virginia. But what captivates me most about Jefferson is how politicians of all political stripes claim him as their own from time to time. Religious conservatives often point to Jefferson's strong belief in God to bolster their desire for a closer relationship between church and state. Those who fear the entanglement of church and state counter that Jefferson openly doubted the divinity of Christ and warned about too close a relationship between organized religion and organized government. Those who favor smaller government, like to bring up how Jefferson believed that the ideal government was a nation of farmers, while those who prefer a stronger central government note that the third president greatly expanded the role of the presidency and the size of the country. Some claim that Jefferson was a man of great morality while others maintain that he had a long-lasting affair with one of his slaves. One aspect of Jefferson's life that can not be debated is that he is an extremely fascinating individual.

The Castleman's Ferry float receives extremely light fishing and boating pressure and offers superlative fishing, canoeing, nature viewing, and photography opportunities. Canoeists will likely find it a marvelous half-day getaway through a pastoral area of the two Virginias, while anglers can easily spend eight or more hours exploring all the fishing hot spots. The beginning of this excursion does not foreshadow what it will become. A powerline crosses the river, boating and fishing are popular near the ramp, and a golf course lies on the river right shoreline. The water is also primarily slow and deep during the first mile. One of the most commonly heard birds along this section is the house wren, an avian more associated with suburbia than the wilds.

At about the two-mile point, a fair size island appears; take the right passageway. Next comes Parker Island, the last major feature before the Virginia/West Virginia line. Either side is passable, but more current exists on the left side, and the river left shoreline, where trees grow in great profusion, provides numerous smallmouth lairs. Canoeists may want to take the right side around Parker for the deeper water. A short distance after you pass Parker Island, you will enter the Mountain State, but there are no signs or markers to make note of that occurrence. Half way into the Castleman's Ferry float, and about a mile into West Virginia, you will come to the first major riffle, which is where Hog Run enters on river right. From Hog Run until the take-out, the fishing action can be non-stop and both banks are heavily wooded with only occasional homes or farms interrupting.

I rank the bass fishing so highly because the habitat is ideal. For example, below Hog Run comes a series of rock ledges, underwater boulders, and riffles. At about the four-mile point come another series of riffles and rocky substrate; this is known as the Riverside area. A Class I rapid then follows as do more riffles in the vicinity of where Long Marsh Run enters from river left. Near the five-mile point, the Main Stem forms a river right curve and more riffles and ledges characterize that locale. And over the next mile, as the Shenandoah flows fairly straight, additional riffles and ledges punctuate the stream. During the last mile of the float, a long river left ledge dominates the scenery and is a great place to stop and take pictures or have a snack. Water willow grows along the ledge, which is well above the water line. Toward the end of the float, you will spot a river left farm and a gravel road running parallel to the Shenandoah. Then come two wide spots in the river left shoreline and a gravel/dirt slide that descends to the river. I always worry about missing this take-out because it is not easy to spot. Despite the poor access to this float, or maybe because of it, the Castleman's Ferry float is one of my favorites in the two Virginias.

Avon Bend to Bloomery Road contains numerous riffles to fish and to send paddlers on their way.

3.6
AVON BEND (MEYER'S FERRY) TO BLOOMERY ROAD

The Essentials

Trip: Avon Bend (Meyer's Ferry) to Bloomery Road, both in Jefferson County. Refer to Map 9 in Appendix C.

USGS Quads: Round Hill and Charles Town

Distance: 8 miles

Rapids: A possible Class II, Is, and riffles

Access Points: At Avon Bend, the river left put-in is a gravel/dirt slide. See "The Essentials" section of the preceding chapter. At Bloomery Road, the river left take-out is a gravel ramp. Parking spaces are numerous in the gravel lot.

One of the seminal events in American and Civil War history was John Brown's capture of the United States Arsenal at Harpers Ferry on October 17, 1859. The abolitionist's goal apparently was that once he and his 18 men were fortified by the arsenal's weapons, they would abscond into the surrounding mountains and encourage slaves to rebel. Brown and his followers were themselves captured the following day by a man whom history would hear from again, Colonel Robert E. Lee. At the trial that followed, many Northerners wanted Brown to be declared insane while Southerners demanded the death penalty, fearing that slave revolts would be the result if Brown were not dealt the ultimate penalty. Dixie's viewpoint won out, Brown was convicted of treason, and on December 2, 1859 he was hanged. The differing opinion concerning Brown was just one of many factors that helped lead to the Civil War in 1861. Today, visitors to Harpers Ferry can learn more about the life of John Brown.

Canoeists will need a full four hours to cover the Avon Bend float while float fishermen can easily spend seven or so hours visiting the best spots. Over the years, I have taken the Avon Bend junket many times, several with my wife, and it remains one of my favorites on the entire Shenandoah system. Gerald Lewis, a West Virginia Division of Natural Resources biologist, says the Main Stem possesses an excellent smallmouth population as well as good numbers of rock bass, redbreast sunfish, and channel catfish. Another reason for my being enamoured with this float is that the birdwatching is always good. On my most recent excursion, I heard or saw Acadian flycatchers, osprey, Louisiana waterthrush, and great blue herons upon launching. During the day, I also caught glimpses of a bald eagle, peewees, green herons, wood ducks, mallards, Canada geese, and some 20 species of other avians.

Not long after putting in, you will come to an island; take the right passageway. The first feature of note is a Class I rapid that occurs about a mile from the put-in. This is a very easy rapid to run, but the best path is on far river right. The push water above this rapid and the eddies and runs below make for excellent fishing opportunities. Also worth noting is a boulder field below the rapid.

The Main Stem then creates a river right bend and more boulders dot the streambed. Soon you will come to another island and a

Class I rapid at its head. The best pathway is down the left side of the island. Most all of the preceding trip was characterized by heavily wooded shorelines, but the Avon Bend float contains many more homes and summer dwellings, especially on river left after this island. The river right shoreline, though, remains cloaked with trees. Next, you will enter a river left bend, signifying that two miles have been covered.

Coming out of this bend, you will soon encounter Fairfax's Falls, a nearly one-mile-long section of Class I rapids and riffles. A brick home on a river left peak helps mark the beginning of Fairfax's Falls, but the best giveaway is the sound of the falls themselves. If you are a fisherman, this section is where I recommend that you spend much of your time. The mid-river smallmouth habitat is excellent with the current breaks and push water, while water willows and sycamores grow along or near the shorelines. Paddlers will find that this section is a delight to run as the current sends them briskly along. On one float through here with guide Frank Baker of River Riders, Frank caught a number of quality brown bass by drifting a twin tail grub below this rapid. Crayfish lures and fly patterns will almost always work in habitat like this.

The first two rapids of Fairfax's Falls are easy Class Is, and then you come to a series of riffles before another Class I occurs near the end of the falls. Small bluffs line the river left shoreline, the last of which marks the end of Fairfax. Next comes some very slow moving water and the Main Stem forms a mild river right bend. Hammond's Ferry, a shallow section, lies in the midst of this bend. The end of the curve is also the five-mile point for the Avon Bend getaway. The river then straightens and slows somewhat and you will pass through what is known as Turkey Bottom. At about the six-mile point, a rock garden comes into view, and this is a super place to fish for smallmouths, especially in the spring before the fish have moved into swift water.

You will then make a river right curve and spot a river right bluff and the Route 9 Bridge. Numerous islets lie on the river left side of the bridge making passage difficult. The best route is on far river right, but a Class II rapid can exist there in the spring. If you decide to portage, the best way is on river right. Some scattered islets and deep-water boulders lie below the bridge for a short distance, but basically the best fishing and floating for this trip are over. Bloomery Road parallels the entire river left shoreline, making the area a haven for bank fishermen. The only problem, though, is that the habitat is generally lacking, especially for larger smallmouths. Catfish anglers should find this section to their liking, however.

After you pass under the bridge, you will have about a mile-and-a-half paddle to reach the take-out. Many people like to take-out about half way through this slow section, which is known as the Big Eddy, on river left at Mouton Park. The park has a large gravel lot and a river left gravel ramp. Or you can continue on to the final take-out, which lies just above a Class II rapid and a powerline. Portaging around the Millville Hydro Dam would result in a boat carry of more than a half-mile. Better to debark above the Class II. As a final note on this chapter, biologist Lewis says that largemouth bass anglers should visit the Big Eddy pool in the spring. Excellent numbers of bass come from this area every year from March through May.

The Bloomery Road excursion has the most whitewater on the Shenandoah system.

3.7
BLOOMERY ROAD TO POTOMAC WAYSIDE

The Essentials

Trip: Bloomery Road (below Millville Dam) in Jefferson County to Potomac Wayside, in Loudon County, Virginia. Refer to Map 9 in Appendix C.

USGS Quads: Round Hill, Charles Town, and Harpers Ferry

Distance: 6 miles

Rapids: A possible Class IV, IIIs, IIs, Is, and riffles

Access Points: On Bloomery Road, a river left put-in exists several hundred yards below the dam. The ramp is gravel, and parking spaces are available in a gravel lot. At Potomac Wayside, the river right take-out is a mud incline. A sign on a post helps mark the access point. A narrow dirt path leads up a hillside to a small gravel parking lot, adjacent to Route 340.

Elaine and I relish staying at bed and breakfasts after we finish floating rivers, and one of our favorites is the Washington House Inn, operated by Mel and Nina Vogel, in Charles Town. Nina says that Charles Town and her inn are at the heart of some Washington family history.

"Charles Town, which was founded in 1786, is named for Charles Washington, brother of George," says Nina. "In Charles' will, he donated 80 acres to the town with the provision that the land be for public use only. Actually, this donation was about the highpoint of Charles' life. He didn't have any major accomplishments and was basically a do nothing."

"In 1899, John and Augusta Washington, George's great grand nephews, built the Washington House Inn and lived in it until 1949. Afterwards, the house was turned into five apartments, later into a single family home, and then fell into a state of disrepair. In 1989, the house became a bed and breakfast, and Mel and I bought the place in 1993. We reopened it in March of 1994. People come to bed and breakfasts to either find beautiful places, good food, or hospitality. When they come here, I want them to find all three."

The Bloomery Road float should only be undertaken by expert canoeists, emphasizes Matt Knott, who operates River Riders in Harpers Ferry. Strong Class III rapids and one possible Class IV exist, making this float the most whitewater-filled one on the entire Shenandoah system. Even in the summer, continues Knott, major drops still exist and are capable of causing even expert paddlers to encounter difficulty. I have taken this float in a ducky and brought along two fishing rods instead of my usual four. Knott says that duckies and kayaks are the best craft for negotiating this section during the summer months when water levels are often low, while rafts are the choice during the spring.

Canoeists and kayakers can zip through the Bloomery Road getaway in three hours or less, while float fishermen may want to spend seven or eight hours. The smallmouth bass habitat is some of the best on the Shenandoah system, and the trip does not receive much fishing pressure because of the many rapids. You will put in across from an island and for several hundred yards have the option of fishing the left side of the island or the river left shoreline. Riffles and plenty of rock cover exist, but this section receives intense fishing pressure from wade and bank fishermen. After you pass the island, the current noticeably slows; and at the one-mile point of the float, you enter a wide river left curve. At the head of the curve, you will notice a pumping station that is releasing water from a quarry. Throughout this first leg of the float, Bloomery Road has paralleled the river left shoreline. For the next mile or so, you will float through a slow-moving, rocky pool that can provide excellent spring action for smallmouths.

Ben Harrison, who is a guide for River Riders, accompanied me on one Bloomery Road float. The Hedgesville resident finds the first two miles of this trip uneventful, but the last four miles anything but. Both of us were in duckies, and these small craft, says Harrison, are ideal for not only maneuvering through fast water but also experiencing whitewater to its utmost. The whitewater begins at the two-mile point. A series of islets and ledges cross the river; take the left path around these formations and you will come to a Class I, Entrance Rapid. (A trail from a campground leads to this point.) Soon afterwards, Bull's Falls looms. Bull's Falls is a series of rapids and can vary from a Class II to III, depending on water levels; the rapid can be portaged on river left. Puff Rock lies hard above the falls. Harrison says to run to the left of Puff Rock and then the rapid itself should be run center right. Second Bull Falls pocks the bottom immediately below and then comes Third Hydraulic. A short distance below appears a Class I to II, which seems almost simple after what exists above. Also note that railroad tracks run along the river left side as does a rock wall. Both banks are part of the Harper's Ferry National Historical Park. This entire area is very photogenic as the combination of hillsides, rapids, islets, and a major drop in the stream bottom are stunning in their beauty. Fly fishermen will find this section great for working streamers and nymphs through the swift water while spin fishermen should do well with crankbaits and grubs. Harrison likes to eat shore lunches on the many boulders that stud the bottom and both shorelines.

Below Bull's Falls lies a long rock garden and numerous riffles and Class Is, giving the whitewater paddler and angler more to look forward to. Several hundred yards below Bull's Falls exists a Class I to

II rapid that includes the remains of a dam. Harrison warns that exposed spikes from the structure stretch across the river and can be
dangerous. Portage on river left if the water is so low that the spikes
present hazards. Next comes another rock garden and more islets,
including a fairly large one on river right. Paddlers will relish exploring
this area while fishermen can practice their craft. The Shenandoah
slows for just a short distance, but by the time you come to the last mile
of the Main Stem, yet another rapid looms—Upper Staircase. Upper
Staircase can range from a Class I to III depending on water levels;
generally, says Harrison, the best path is on the left when the river is
low. However, under normal to high water levels, the guide suggests
negotiating Upper Staircase on far river right.

Route 340 crosses the Shenandoah and separates Upper Staircase from Lower Staircase, which is a Class I to II for the most part.
During low flows, Harrison recommends that Lower Staircase be run on
its far river left side. On the river right side is the Class III to IV
Heaven's Gate, which is part of Lower Staircase; this rapid features
what Harrison labels a "huge hydraulic." Portage on river left. The
guide also maintains that Heaven's Gate is easier to run when water
levels are high; its rocks and ledges are underwater then.

After your break free of Upper and Lower Staircase, a majestic
cliff greets you in the distance, steep hillsides envelope the river, and
you see the remains of bridge supports. Thomas Jefferson was so
enamoured with this vista that he penned the following words: "This
scene is worth a voyage across the Atlantic." I agree and was thrilled
when I passed several river-right boulders at the mouth of the
Shenandoah and entered the Potomac. While I was congratulating
myself, and giving thanks to God, for having floated the entire lengths
of the James, New, Rappahannock, South Fork of the Shenandoah, and
Main Stem of the Shenandoah, Ben Harrison interrupted my reverie and
warned that the mile to the take-out flaunts some very intense rapids.

First, you will pass through an easy Class I, but then the
Potomac's substrate drops precipitously. Stretching across the river in a
row are the Class I to II Wake Up (which should be run on river left),
the Class III+ White Horse (with the "+" side being on the left and
dangerous hydraulics in the center), and the Class III Washing Machine

(which should be run on the far left). My advice is to portage this entire section on river left, which is also the side that the C&O Canal parallels. After surviving these rapids, move over to the river-right shoreline and look for a pole with a sign atop that says "Potomac Wayside." Piney Run enters here, next to a dirt slide take-out. You have now ended your voyage down the Shenandoah system.

Part Four
Rappahannock River

John Garman taking a break from canoeing to fish a pool on the Remington float.

4.1
REMINGTON TO KELLY'S FORD

The Essentials

Trip: Remington in Fauquier County to Kelly's Ford in Culpepper County. Refer to Map 10 in Appendix C.

USGS Quads: Remington and Germanna Bridge

Distance: 4½ miles

Rapids: A Class III, IIs, Is, and riffles

Access Points: At Remington, the river left put-in is a few yards above the Route 15 Bridge. You will have to slide your boat down a narrow, steep, dirt trail. Parking consists of a roadside pull-off next to a river gage. At Kelly's Ford, the river right take-out is at a wooden step/canoe slide ramp below the Route 620 (Kelly's Ford Road) Bridge via Route 651 (Summerduck Road). Parking spaces are numerous in the gravel lot.

Certainly some of the bloodiest and most crucial battles of the Civil War occurred in the Rappahannock River area. The Battle of Chancellorsville, which took place from May 1-4, 1863, went down in the history books as a victory for the Confederates and their leader, General Robert E. Lee. But the Chancellorsville victory certainly qualified as a Pyrrhic one for the South. During the conflict, General Lee, who led only some sixty thousand men, went against the one hundred thirty-eight thousand troops of General Joseph Hooker. The key to the victory was when Lee and General Stonewall Jackson moved on Hooker's forces from the front and right flank, respectively. Brilliant moves, to be sure, by Lee and Jackson, but one that resulted in tragedy. Jackson's own forces shot him accidentally, causing the general's arm to be amputated; and on May 10, Stonewall died from complications. Lee's famous quote was as follows: "He has lost his left arm, but I have lost my right arm."

The Remington float will only take a few hours for paddlers, and float fishermen can easily negotiate it in four to six hours. The trip is one of stark contrasts; the first three miles feature very slow moving water and scattered rocks along the shoreline and the bottom. The last mile and a half consists of a rock garden with many rapids, some of which can be dangerous to run during high water conditions. *Note: Only expert canoeists should attempt this float during high water conditions.* After the put-in, you will drift under the Route 15 Bridge and then run an easy Class I/riffle above a railroad bridge. You will also pass a stone wall on river left. After Tin-Pot Run enters on river right, the scenery will vary little for the next three miles. Scattered houses, a sandy bottom, high banks on both sides of the river, and numerous downed trees greet the paddler. The sameness of the surroundings, however, should not make them sound unappealing.

I simply love this section of the Remington junket. On a trip with John Garman, who along with Bill Micks operates the Virginia Outdoor Center in Fredericksburg, we observed a bald eagle, several ospreys, and a host of avians such as Eastern kingbirds, great blue herons, green herons, and common yellowthroats. I also dueled with three 20-inch smallmouths, all of which hit topwater lures. The first trophy smallie smashed a Rapala Skitter Prop and after leaping twice and scraping my line against an underwater boulder, then wrapped itself around a submerged tree limb. The smallie finally broke the line and then leaped again as a final insult. The next 20-incher clobbered another topwater bait, a Storm Chug Bug, and performed similar escape routines, including wrapping itself around an underwater tree limb three times. John had to debark from the boat and unwrap the line in order to lip the bass. I ended up losing another 20-inch brown bass while we were floating through the rock garden. The fishing potential of the Remington float is obvious.

At about the two-mile-mark, you will pass through a riffle and a mile later, you will float past scattered boulders and a deep pool below; this is a clue that the rock garden is imminent. Garman, who has made the Remington float many times in all seasons, says that rapids in the rock garden can range from Class I to III, depending on water levels. The rock garden, which features remains from Wheatley's Canal, has, as its major drop, the Sandy Beach Rapid. In high water, you will have to make two quick turns when running Sandy Beach, which is named for the sandy beach that lies below the rapid on river left. My advice is to portage Sandy Beach Rapid on river left. The other rapids can be simple Class Is, but they also can decrease to riffles during the low water of summer or increase to Class IIs during heavy rains or winter runoff.

Besides the Sandy Beach rapid, two other features stand out in the rock garden. Both of these are stone walls that lie on river left; they are separated by several hundred yards and occur in the last half-mile of the float. The bridge at Kelly's Ford comes into view when you have about a quarter-mile left. This trip is short, but it is well worth your time.

The confluence of the Rapidan and Rappahannock is a popular place to fish, take pictures, and camp.

4.2
KELLY'S FORD TO MOTTS RUN LANDING

The Essentials

Trip: Kelly's Ford in Fauquier and Culpepper counties to Motts Run Landing in Stafford and Spotsylvania counties. Refer to Map 11 in Appendix C.

USGS Quads: Remington. Germanna Bridge, Richardsville, Storck, Chancellorsville, and Salem Church

Distance: 24½ miles

Rapids: Class IIs, Is, and riffles

Access Points: At Kelly's Ford, the river right put-in is at a wooden step/canoe slide ramp below the Route 620 Bridge (Kelly's Ford Road) via Route 651 (Summerduck Road). Parking spaces are numerous in the gravel lot. At Motts Run Landing, the river right take-out is at a wooden step/canoe slide ramp off Route 618 (River Road). Parking spaces are numerous in the gravel lot. Clore Brothers Canoe Livery lies immediately downstream on river right.

143

The Founding Fathers such as Washington, Adams, Franklin, and Jefferson often find themselves the subjects of books and documentaries. But our fifth president, James Monroe, rarely receives such acclaim. That's too bad because Monroe's contributions to the young country are quite impressive. The native Virginian fought in the Revolutionary War, was elected to the Congress of the Confederation, and was a diplomat under President Jefferson. But his crowning achievement came as president, the Monroe Doctrine. The doctrine basically proclaimed that the United States would not allow foreign countries to create new colonies in the Western Hemisphere. The James Monroe Museum on Charles Street in Fredericksburg is an excellent place to learn more about this son of the Old Dominion.

I must confess that this float is the reason why I have penned river guides on the James, New, and Shenandoah and Rappahannock. Back in the 1980s, my wife Elaine and I floated the Rappahannock for the first time, taking the 24½-mile excursion from Kelly's Ford to Motts Landing. We had no river guidebooks to help determine where we were, and we constantly speculated about how many miles we had covered. By the second day, my wife became convinced that we had missed the take-out, and we paddled furiously trying to reach civilization of some kind. We ended up arriving at Motts Landing *eight hours ahead of schedule*, to our great embarrassment. I remarked to Elaine that some day someone needed to write guidebooks on the Rappahannock and the other major streams in Virginia. Today, whenever we are on the James, New, Shenandoah, or Rappahannock and Elaine questions me about where we are and how many miles we have covered, I always say: "Darling, *I wrote the book* on this river, trust me." And she does, or at least I think she does. The Kelly's Ford float is best taken as a two-day excursion for paddlers and a three-day affair for float fishermen. This trip is, in my opinion, the most beautiful one in Virginia and West Virginia; and it always amazes me how fortunate this section of the Rappahannock has been to have escaped the development that has so ravaged the landscape of Northern Virginia. (See the Introduction for an explanation of the Rappahannock's good fortune.)

At the beginning of the Kelly's Ford float, an island cleaves the river, take the left route. A set of riffles lies below the island and then the river flows very gently for the first mile. As is true with the previous getaway, this trip also features very similar habitat. High banks dominate both shorelines, a sandy bottom is the norm, and trees crowd both banks, giving one a glimpse into the river's past. Surely, paddlers from previous centuries must have enjoyed similar vistas. The major indicator of man's presence are the rock walls left from the river's canal era. Just past the one-mile mark, you will come to a small island; take the left passageway. Occasional small islets will then appear, all of them covered with water willows. The next major feature is the ruins from Mountain Run Dam; a Class I forms here and plenty of passages exist. At the 2½-mile point, Mountain Run enters on river right. The Rap flows fairly straight for the next mile until you come to an island, which is a popular place for campers. Riffles and a gentle Class I lie above the island and more of the same occurs when you take the right passageway around the island. Flat water exists below the island and continues, except for the occasional riffle, until the six-mile point. The occasional farm on river left also characterizes this portion of the river.

At the six-mile mark, the ruins from Kemper's Ford Dam dot the river and create a Class I. Below these ruins, the gradient noticeably increases. The smallmouth angling has been quite acceptable so far, but it becomes even better. Streamers stripped through these riffles should produce plenty of fish as should 3-inch grubs on jigheads. In fact, on a float with good friend Rick Moorer of Roanoke, I once caught an 18 and a 20-inch smallmouth with grubs. At about the seven-mile point, the farms end and the wooded shoreline on river left returns.

One of my favorite sections of the Rappahannock is next on the agenda. First you will pass through a series of riffles and then come to the old Snake Castle Canal, which was constructed for batteaux. The canal lies at about the eight-mile point on river right. Across the Rap exists the ruins from Snake Castle Dam. Below these two features, appears an island; take the right passageway for some outstanding fishing and paddling. Riffles dot the passage as does a Class II at the lower end. On river left, be sure to note Snake Castle Rock, a large outcropping that is a great place to stop to take photos and have a shorelunch on a sandbar. I recall a very memorable float through here with my wife and Bill Micks. We ate turkey sandwiches and chatted while watching canoeists attempt to negotiate the Class II, one couple overturned part way through this rapid. (Portage on river left or right.) Also look for damsel and dragonflies flitting about the many water willow beds in this area. If a hatch of these creatures is occurring, the fly and spinfishing can be tremendous. The riffles below the island also create fishing opportunities.

At the nine-mile point, some more riffles appear and then Summerduck Run enters on river left. Below Summerduck Run, you will drift by Martin's Ford and then course by a series of islets; easy Class Is and riffles proffer more angling and paddling recreation. This section ends when Rock Run enters on river left. The next major feature is the Rappahannock River Campground, which is located at the end of Route 683, on river right; you have now covered about 11 miles. Below is Crawley's Dam ruins, which form another of the riffles or Class Is so characteristic of this waterway. At the 12-mile point, Deep Run enters on river left and you will come to an island in a river left curve; take the right passageway. For the next nearly two miles, only the occasional riffle sends you along your way. But then you come to the remains of Lock 13 that is situated next to a river right bluff.

At this point, I must confess to an angling blunder that I have made many times on Kelly's Ford floats. From Lock 13 (and the maze of rocks below it) and the three miles to the confluence, in my opinion, the best smallmouth habitat on the Rappahannock exists. But almost every time I have canoed the river, I have spent so much time fishing that usually little daylight is left at this stage. The best places to camp are at the confluence of the Rappahannock and Rapidan or just down-stream. So as darkness has approached, I have had to paddle a lot and cast little in order to make camp before sunset. Try to budget your fishing time so that you don't commit my snafu.

I am not going to mindlessly repeat that good fishing exists at every rapid and rock structure from now to the confluence, though such is the case. Here, though, is what you will encounter. Below Lock 13, you will see the ruins of Powell's Dam, more riffles, and then an island where people like to camp. Take the left passageway and note Richland Run entering on river left. Below, the river makes a short river left and then river-right curve, and the shoreline fishing can be outstanding as shadows lengthen across the river. From upstream, you will soon notice a rock garden and a power line crossing the river. You will also hear the roar of the Rappahannock and Rapidan coming together and the Class II rock garden that exists at the end of the Rapidan and at and below the confluence.

The river-right point at the confluence is where I have spent a number of nights. Camping where two rivers commingle is always a pleasant experience. John Garman of the Virginia Outdoor Center is a master at planning multiple trips down the Rappahannock. Watching John set up a tent in just a few minutes and preparing a gourmet meal in an equally short time is a pleasant memory from one of my Rappahannock trips.

For those delicate of spirit, modesty compels me to mention that this area is the haunt of the "Confluence Streaker," an older gentleman who likes to appear and bathe in the buff. My wife Elaine describes the man as being "not a pretty sight." Be forewarned.

Bill Micks warns that the Class II rock garden can metamorphose into a Class III during high water conditions. From personal experience, I agree. On one trip, Elaine and I ventured onto the Rapidan on a proposed two-day float that would cover both rivers. But an intense thunderstorm came and the river quickly rose and became muddy. By the time we arrived at the confluence, part of the rock garden had Class III rapids to contend with. At one of those rapids, we kissed a rock and overturned our canoe, losing much of our gear. We then had to seek shelter on river right while the storm subsided. Knowing that even higher water was likely on its way, my spouse and I quickly paddled the eight miles to Motts Run Landing. It was a good thing we did because the rains continued into the night. The next day, the Rappahannock was at flood level. Be sure to contact outfitters and view the Weather Channel before planning a float, sound advice for any river trip.

Below the confluence, you will note two boulders that are vertical to the stream bottom. Bill Micks calls these "Clapping Rock." Next comes a small island and the usual riffles, as well as a Class I at the lower end. There are also some stone walls on river right that are popular places to camp. After a series of riffles and Class Is, you will pass Blankenbaker's Farm on river right and a gas line. This is a very flat section, which is a nice respite considering what lies above. You also have now covered about 18 miles. Soon you will come to a Class I/riffle, which is followed by a river right bend, both of which provide angling opportunities. I have been concentrating on the smallmouth fishing until now, but the river sports a very good redbreast sunfish population, informs Virginia Department of Game and Inland Fisheries biologist, John Odenkirk. He adds that rock bass also fin the river in good numbers. So if you are interested in numbers of fish, downsize your flies and lures and have a ball with the panfish.

Below the river right bend lies Porch's Lock, which creates a series of riffles. For the next mile, the Rap flows fairly straight until you come to about the 20-mile point. The river then forms a long, looping river left bend that has riffles and one Class I, near where Horsepen Run enters on river left. After you leave the bend, the next major feature is the Ballard's Dam ruins where a Class I dots the river. Then come more riffles and small islands for the next two miles or so. For the last mile and a half, the Kelly's Ford float is fairly flat with the only important features being where Rocky Pen Run enters on river left and where Sanford's Ferry crosses. Motts Run Landing is a welcome sight, but my what a trip this one is.

The Mott's Run Landing getaway is an underutilized float on the Rappahannock.

4.3
MOTTS RUN LANDING TO OLD MILL PARK

The Essentials

Trip: Motts Run Landing to Old Mill Park in Stafford and Spotsylvania counties. Refer to Map 12 in Appendix C.

USGS Quads: Salem Church and Fredericksburg

Distance: 6 miles

Rapids: A Class III, IIs, Is, and riffles

Access Points: At Motts Run Landing, the river right put-in is at a wooden step/canoe slide ramp off Route 618 (River Road). Parking spaces are numerous in the gravel lot. Clore Brothers Canoe Livery lies immediately downstream on river right. The river right take-out is off Caroline Street at Old Mill Park. No ramp exists; you will have to pull your craft across some rocks and up a short incline at the park. Parking spaces are numerous in the gravel lot.

149

How much about our Founding Fathers is fact and how much is fiction? Supposedly, two of the questionable "facts" concerning George Washington took place on Ferry Farm, just outside of Fredericksburg. It was there that the father of our country supposedly said, "I cannot tell a lie," when his own father asked him who had cut down a cherry tree. Washington's admission of guilt was a small matter compared to his supposedly hurling a silver dollar across the Rappahannock from Ferry Farm. I am not going to pass judgement on the cherry tree affair, but I doubt that old G.W. could have tossed a dollar across the Rappahannock, unless he were far upstream from the Remington put-in.

At this writing, one major factor affects whether or not the Motts Run Landing float is a stupendous one or just an average one. Embrey Dam was supposed to have been removed by the turn of the century, but all kinds of delays have pushed the project's completion back, possibly as late as February 2006. State fisheries biologist John Odenkirk says that the smallmouth bass on the Rappahannock have slower growth rates than those on the James, New, and Shenandoah systems. If the dam is eventually removed, and shad are once again allowed to run up the river as they historically did, the bass fishery may be greatly enhanced. And paddlers and float fishermen will not have to endure a miserable portage around a dam that no longer serves a purpose.

That said, the Motts Run float is a four-hour junket for paddlers and a six-hour trip for float fishermen. Neither time allotment takes into account the portage. Soon after launching, you will spot the water intake for Motts Run Reservoir on river right. The gray stone building and its gate valves are highly visible. If a siren sounds for water release, quickly paddle away from that shoreline and go downstream. Before you come to a river right bend, you will see a cable and a series of islets in the bend. A Class I rapid and riffles characterize this area as well.

After leaving the bend, don't be surprised to espy some climbers scaling a river right cliff; this is a very popular local haunt. Then looms "The Maze," a quarter-mile long rock garden that features several possible Class Is, plus numerous riffles. Flat water is the norm for nearly a mile until you come to the remains of Taylor's Dam, which creates riffles and gentle Class Is. At just past the three-mile point, you will pass under Interstate 95 and riffles exist both above and below the bridge. What you encounter next will depend on whether or not Embrey Dam has been removed. Bill Micks says that significant Class II-III rapids could re-emerge after the dam is destroyed. John Garman states the resulting rapids could be enthusiastically greeted by whitewater fans and thus cause tourism dollars to enter the city of Fredericksburg. Fishermen may find the smallmouth action outstanding. But as for now, Embrey Dam results in a tedious river left portage.

The Virginia Outdoor Center lies several hundred yards below the dam on river right, and clients of the business often debark from the river there. A winding path leads from the river to the business' headquarters. And an informal take-out lies just downstream on river right off Fall Hill Avenue. This access point is nothing more than a wide opening in the bank, and parking is very limited.

Obviously, a reason exists for why paddlers and anglers might want to take out before the end of the trip, even though the float has more than a mile to run. That reason is the Laucks Island rock garden, which begins just below Embrey Dam. I have paddled the half-mile venture along the right side of Laucks Island with John Garman, who is one of the best canoeists I have ever had the pleasure to go down a river with. Even with John being an expert paddler, we still had a difficult time negotiating the rock garden on a July trip. Water levels were quite low and we walked as much as we paddled. Conversely, says Garman, the rock garden can be very dangerous to run when water levels are high. A series of Class Is form and then First Drop occurs, which John classifies as a Class II to III rapid. When you come to the end of the island, Second Drop punctuates the Rappahannock, and this rapid is a solid Class II. Soon to come are more rapids—Corner, a Class I to II; Becky's Hole Rapid, which can be a Class I to III; and Washing Machine, a Class I to II. John adds that it is very difficult to tell people how to run these rapids, which occur at the fall line of the Rappahannock. Whether or not they are dangerous is so dependent on water levels and current speed. Once again, this is another time to remind readers to obtain current stream information before venturing forth. Finally, a half-mile or so below Laucks Island you will leave the rock garden, near where you pass under the Route 1 Bridge. A few minutes of paddling will bring you to the Old Mill Park take-out. The trip actually ends at the beginning of the tidal Rappahannock.

It was a very emotional time for me when I finished doing the research and all the paddling for the Rappahannock and Shenandoah rivers. I am proud to have paddled the entire lengths of the South Fork, Main Stem of the Shenandoah, and Rappahannock. I hope this guide will benefit you in your quest to learn more about these three remarkable waterways.

APPENDIX A

Guides, Canoe Liveries, Maps, and More

South Fork of the Shenandoah
Downriver Canoe Company
P.O. Box 10
Bentonville, VA 22610
800-338-1963

Front Royal Canoe Company
P.O. Box 473
Front Royal, VA 222630
800-270-8808
www.frontroyalcanoe.com

Shenandoah River Outfitters
6502 S. Page Valley Road
Luray, VA 22835
800-6CANOE2
www.shenandoah-river.com

Shenandoah River Trips
P.O. Box 145
Bentonville, VA 22610
800-RAPIDS-1
www.shenandoah.cc.com

Main Stem of the Shenandoah (West Virginia)
Blue Ridge Outfitters
P.O. Box 750
Harpers Ferry, WV 25425
304-725-3444

River and Trail Outfitters
604 Valley Road
Knoxville, Maryland 21758
888.I-GOPLAY or 301-695-5177
www.rivertrail.com

River Riders
RR 5, Box 1260
Harpers, Ferry, WV 25425
800-326-RAFT
www.riverriders.com

Fishing Guides (Shenandoah System)

Blue Ridge Angler (Billy Kingsley)
1887 South Main Street
Harrisonburg, VA 22801
800-304-8675

Tim Freeze
43195 Parkers Ridge Road
Leesburg, VA 20176-5135
703-443-9052

Lou Kalina
127 N. Jefferson Street
Staunton, VA 24401
540-886-9344

Jeff Kelble
635 North Vermont Street, #2
Arlington, VA 22203
703-243-5389

Shenandoah Lodge (Alec Burnett)
S. Page Valley Road
Luray, VA 22835
800-866-9958
flyfish@shentel.net

John Tipton
Royal Oaks
45 Royal Oaks Lane
Love, VA 22952
800-410-0627

Two Dogs Trading Company (Tom Sadler)
6429 Lambdon Road
The Plains, VA 20198-2054
540-253-7430 or 454-1990

Captain Jack West
209 Boyd Street
Johnson City, TN 37604
423-926-8539

Rappahannock River
Clore Brothers
5927 River Road
Fredericksburg, VA 22407
800-704-7749

Rappahannock Angler at Outdoor Adventures (outdoor supplies)
Smith Coleman, fishing guide (rapangler@msn.com)
4721 Plank Rd.
Fredericksburg, VA 22407
540-786-3334
800-357-9710

Rappahannock River Campground
33017 River Mill Road
Richardsville, VA 22736
800-784-7235
www.canoecamp.com

Virginia Outdoor Center
3219 Fall Hill Avenue
Fredericksburg, VA 22401
877-PLAY-VA2
www.playva.com

LICENSE AND FISHING REGULATION
Virginia Department of Game and Inland Fisheries
P.O. Box 11104
Richmond, VA 23230-1104
804-367-1000
www.dgif.state.va.us

West Virginia Division of Natural Resources
1900 Kanawha Blvd. East
Charleston, WV 25305
304-558-2771
www.dnr.state.wv.us

MAP INFORMATION
Free river maps on the South Fork, the Main Stem in Virginia, and the
Rappahannock are available from the Virginia Department of Game and
Inland Fisheries.

For maps on CD ROM, contact MAPTECH:
635 Portsmouth Avenue
Greenland, NH 03840
(800) 627-7236

Virginia Atlas & Gazetteer and *West Virginia Atlas & Gazetteer*, available from DeLorme Mapping Company, P.O. Box 298, Freeport, ME 04032 (800) 227-1656. The DeLorme publications are the best I have found for negotiating the backroads that often lead to access points.

The Rappahannock Scenic River Atlas and *The Shenandoah River Atlas*, VCNS Sales, Rt. 2, Box 254, Lexington, VA 24450 (540) 463-6777. These are essential publications, and ones that I rely on heavily, for floating the entire lengths of the Shenandoah and Rappahannock systems. Historical information is also included as well as a wealth of other information. The Virginia Canals and Navigations Society (VCNS) is a very worthwhile one, and I am a member. Among its goals are to preserve and enhance Virginia's inland waterways heritage in all its aspects. For information on joining, contact the VCNS, 6826 Rosemont Dr., McLean, VA 22101 (703-356-4027).

TOURISM SOURCES (Rappahannock)
Fredericksburg Area Tourism
4704 Southpoint Parkway
Fredericksburg, VA 22407
800-654-4118
www.fredericksburgvirginia.net

Fredericksburg Visitors Center
706 Caroline St.
Fredericksburg, VA 22401
800-678-4708

TOURISM SOURCES (Shenandoah System)
Front Royal Visitor's Center
414 E. Main St.
Front Royal, VA 22630
800-338-2576
www.frontroyalchamber.com

Jefferson County Convention & Visitors Bureau
P.O. Box A
Harpers, Ferry, WV 25425
800-848-TOUR

Luray-Page Co. Chamber of Commerce
46 E. Main St.
Luray, VA 22835
888-743-3915
www.luraypage.com

Martinsburg-Berkeley County Convention & Visitors Bureau
208 S. Queen St.
Martinsburg, VA 25401
800-498-2386
www.travelwv.com

Roanoke Valley Convention & Visitors Bureau
114 Market St., SE
Roanoke, VA 24011
800-635-5535

Shenandoah County Tourism
600 N. Main St.
Suite 101
Woodstock, VA 22664
888-459-6267
www.shenandoahtravel.org

Shenandoah Travel Council
888-637-3961
www.shenandoahtravel.com

Shenandoah Valley Travel Association
P.O. Box 1040
Dept.TG98
New Market, VA 22844
877-VISIT-SV
www.svta.org

Staunton Convention & Visitors Bureau
116 W. Beverly St.
Staunton, VA 24401
800-332-5219
www.stauntonva.org

Winchester-Frederick County Chamber-CVB
1360 S. Pleasant Valley Rd.
Winchester, VA 22601
800-662-1360
www.visitwinchesterva.com

LODGING

Bavarian Inn and Lodge
Route 1, Box 30
Shepherdstown, WV 25443
304-876-9355
www.bavarianinnwv.com

Belle Grae Inn
515 W. Frederick St.
Staunton, VA 24401
888-541-5151
www.bellegrae.com

Caledonia Farm-1812
Fodderstack Rd.
Flint Hill, VA 22627
800-BNB-1812
www.bnb-n-va.com/cale1812.htm

Carriage Inn
417 E. Washinton St.
Charles Town, WV 25414
800-867-9830
www.carriageinn.com

Chester House Inn
43 Chester St.
Front Royal, VA 22630
800-621-0441
www.chesterhouse.com

Hillbrook Inn
Route 2, Box 152
Charles Town, WV 25414
800-304-4223
www.hillbrookinn.com

Littlepage Inn
15701 Monrovia Rd.
Mineral, VA 23117
800-248-1803
www.littlepage.com

Milton House B&B Inn
P.O. Box 366
Stanley, VA 22851
800-816-3731
www.miltonhouse-inn.com

Mountain Lake Lodge
Rt 2, Box 406
Harpers Ferry, WV 25425
866-ML-Lodge
www.themountainlakelodge.com

Shenandoah Oaks B&B
RR 4, Box 238
Charles Town, WV 25414
304-725-6244
www.shenandoahoaks-wv.com

Tanglewood
P.O. Box 1116
Front Royal, VA 22630
888-635-1411
www.tanglewoodinn.com

The Inn at Narrow Passage
P.O. Box 608
Woodstock, VA 22664
800-459-8002
www.innatnarrowpassage.com

The Inn at Keezletown Rd.
1224 Keezletown Rd.
Weyers Cave, VA 24486
800-465-0100
www.keezlinn.com

Stonewall Jackson Inn (also offers fishing trips)
547 E. Market St.
Harrisonburg, VA 22801
800-445-53330
www.stonewalljacksoninn.com

Washington House Inn
216 S. George St.
Colonial Charles Town, WV 25414
800-297-6957
www.washingtonhouseinnwv.com

Woodward House on Manor Grade
413 S. Royal Ave.
Front Royal, VA 22630
800-635-7011
www.acountryhome.com

STATE PARK

Raymond R. "Andy" Guest, Jr. Shenandoah River State Park
540-622-6840
www.dcr.state.va.us

CONSERVATION

Friends of the Rappahannock
(Private, non-profit advocacy organization)
P.O. Box 7254
Fredericksburg, VA 22404
540-373-3448

Friends of the Shenandoah River
(Private, non-profit advocacy organization)
P.O. Box 410
Front Royal, VA 22630
540-636-4948

Virginia Outdoors Foundation
203 Governor St.
Suite 317
Richmond, VA 23219
804-225-2147
www.virginiaoutdoorsfoundation.com

HELPFUL WEBSITES

The Middle Atlantic River Forecast Center
http://marfchp/.met.psu.edu/

Riversmallies.com (site devoted to river smallmouth fishing)

Virginia District Real Time Streamflow Data
http://water.usgs.gov/realtime.html
or waterdata.usgs.gov/va/hwis/current/?type=flow

West Virginia Current Streamflow Conditions
www.-wv.er.usgs.gov/rt-cgi/gen_tbl_pg?page+5

APPENDIX B

A checklist of birds possibly seen on the Shenandoah and Rappahannock from Spring through Fall.

The form and order of this list follows the Virginia Society of Ornithology format. For more information on bird watching and the seasonal ranges of birds, consult field guides such as those published by Audubon and Peterson.

Heron, Great Blue
Heron, Green
Egret, Great
Heron Yellow-crowned
Goose, Canada
Mallard
Duck, Wood
Vulture, Turkey
Hawk, Sharp-shinned
Hawk, Cooper's
Hawk, Red-tailed
Hawk, Broad-winged
Eagle, Bald
Osprey
Kestrel, American
Grouse, Ruffed
Bobwhite
Turkey
Killdeer
Sandpiper, Spotted
Dove, Rock
Dove, Mourning
Cuckoo, Yellow-billed
Owl, Screech
Owl, Great Horned
Owl, Barred

Chuck-Will's-Widow
Whip-Poor-Will
Nighthawk, Common
Swift, Chimney
Hummingbird, Ruby-throated
Kingfisher, Belted
Flicker, Common
Woodpecker, Pileated
Woodpecker, Red-bellied
Woodpecker, Downy
Flycatcher, Great Crested
Phoebe, Eastern
Flycatcher, Acadian
Pewee, Eastern Wood
Swallow, Tree
Swallow, Bank
Swallow, Rough-winged
Swallow, Barn
Jay, Blue
Raven, Common
Crow, Common
Chickadee, Carolina
Titmouse, Tufted
Nuthatch, White-breasted
Wren, House
Wren, Carolina

Mockingbird
Catbird, Gray
Thrasher, Brown
Robin, American
Thrush, Wood
Thrush, Hermit
Bluebird, Eastern
Gnatcatcher, Blue-gray
Kinglet, Golden-crowned
Kinglet, Ruby-throated
Waxwing, Cedar
Starling
Vireo, White-eyed
Vireo, Yellow-throated
Vireo, Solitary
Vireo, Red-eyed
Vireo, Warbling
Warbler, Black-and-white
Warbler, Worm-eating
Warbler, Northern Parula
Warbler, Yellow
Warbler, Black-throated Green
Warbler, Yellow-throated
Warbler, Pine
Warbler, Prairie
Ovenbird
Waterthrush, Louisiana
Yellowthroat, Common
Chat, Yellow-breasted
Warbler, Hooded
Redstart, American
Meadowlark, Eastern
Blackbird, Red-winged
Oriole, Orchard
Oriole, Baltimore
Grackle, Common

Cowbird, Brown-headed
Tanager, Scarlet
Cardinal
Grosbeak, Rose-breasted
Bunting, Indigo
Goldfinch, American
Towhee, Rufous-sided
Bunting, Indigo
Sparrow, Grasshopper
Junco, Dark-eyed
Sparrow, Chipping
Sparrow, Field
Sparrow, Song

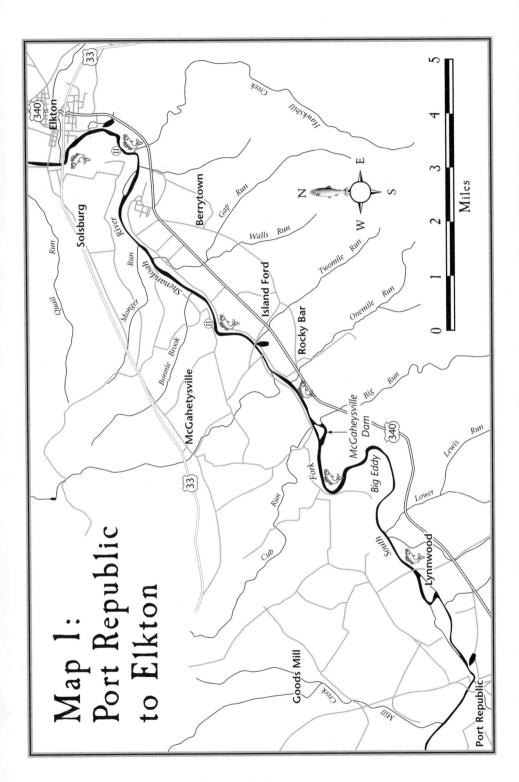

Map 1:
Port Republic
to Elkton

Quail Run

Solsburg

Elkton

33

340

11

Shenandoah River

Monger Run

Bonnie Brook

McGahetysville

33

Berrytown

Gap Run

Walls Run

Island Ford

Rocky Bar

Fork

Cub Run

Run

Goods Mill

Creek

Mill

Port Republic

Lynnwood

South

Big Eddy

McGaheysville Dam

340

Big Run

Twomile Run

Onemile Run

Lewis Run

Lower

Hawksbill Creek

11

N
E
W
S

0   1   2   3   4   5
Miles

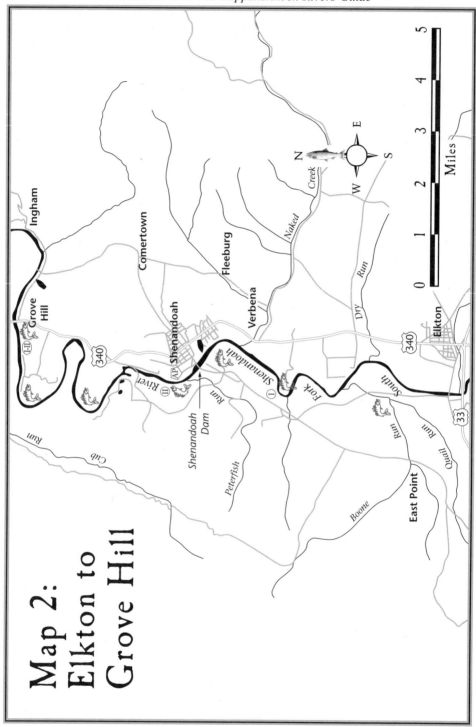

Map 2:
Elkton to
Grove Hill

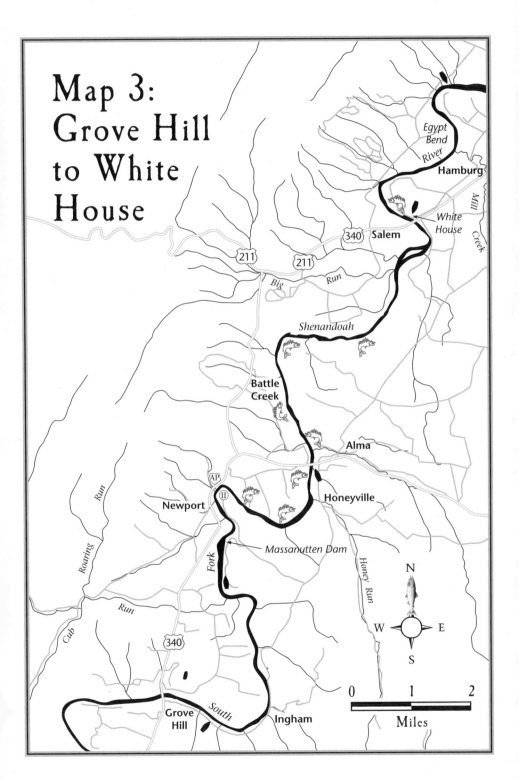

Map 3:
Grove Hill
to White
House

Egypt
Bend

River

Hamburg

Mill Creek

340 Salem

White
House

211

211

Big Run

Shenandoah

Battle
Creek

Alma

AP

II

Newport

Honeyville

Fork

Massanutten Dam

Run

Honey Run

Roaring

N

Run

W E

Cub

Run

S

340

0 1 2

Grove
Hill

South

Ingham

Miles

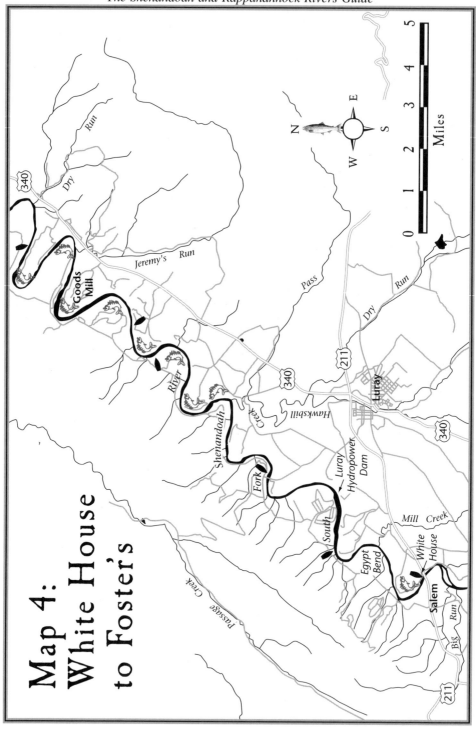

Map 4:
White House
to Foster's

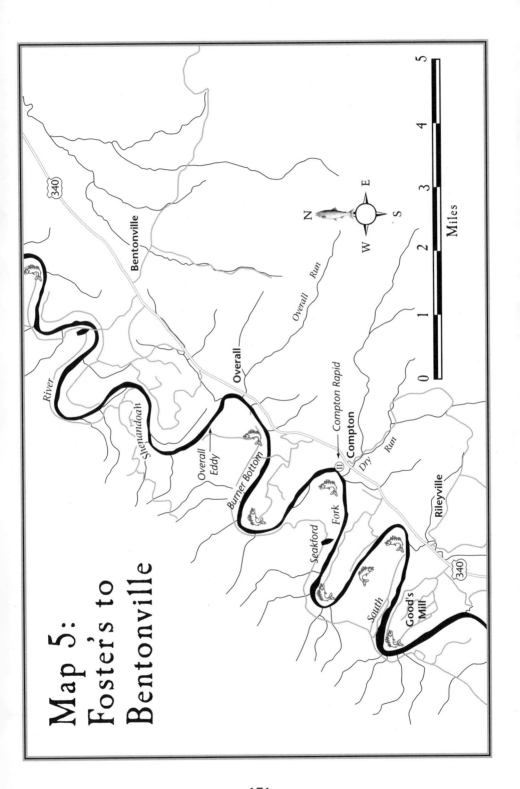

Map 5:
Foster's to
Bentonville

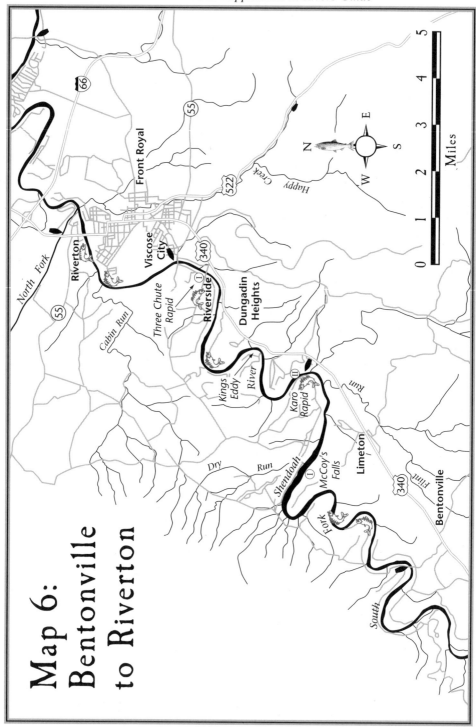

Map 6:
Bentonville
to Riverton

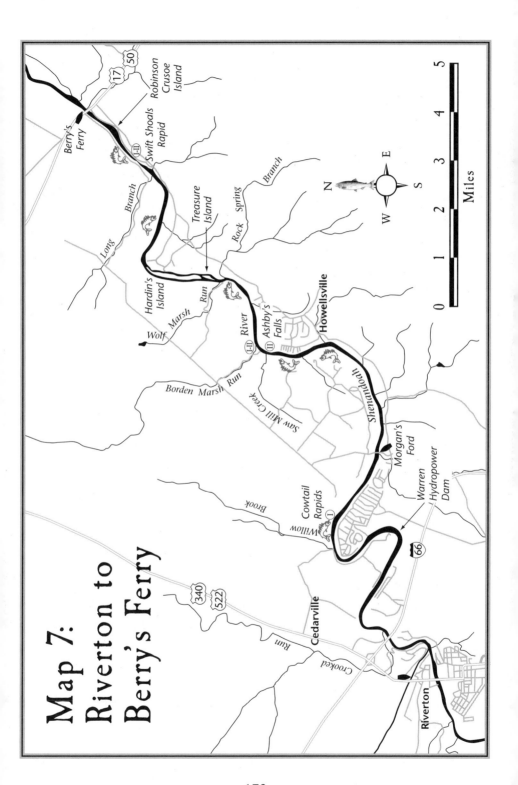

Map 7:
Riverton to
Berry's Ferry

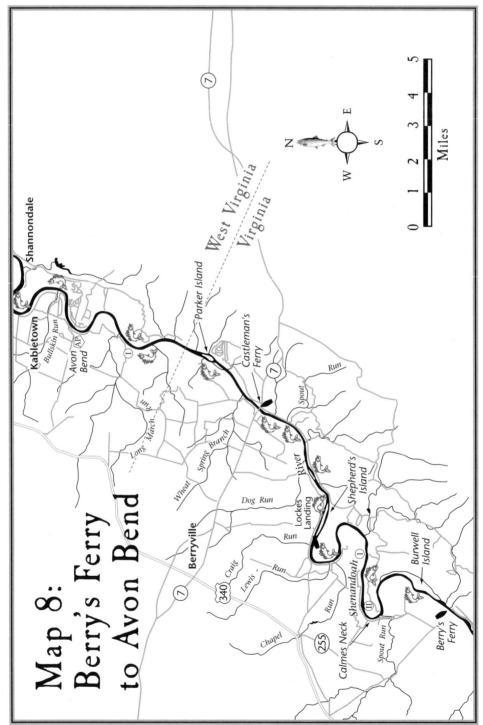

Map 8:
Berry's Ferry
to Avon Bend

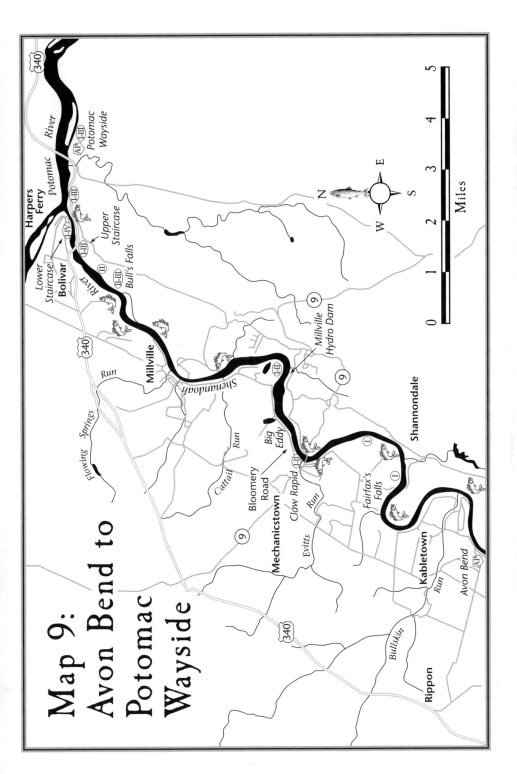

Map 9:
Avon Bend to
Potomac Wayside

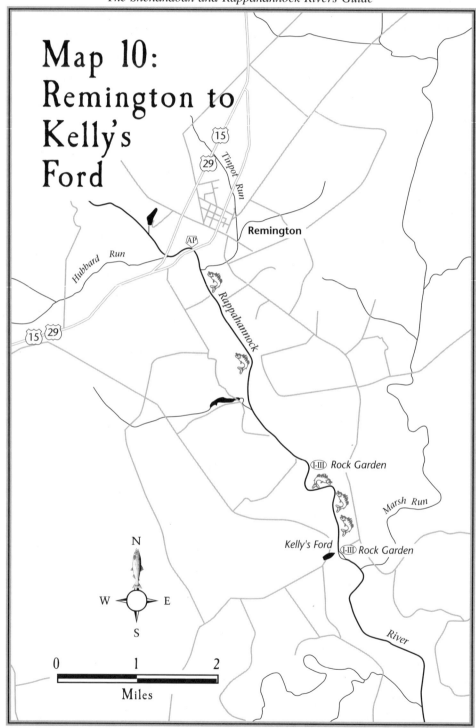

Map 10:
Remington to
Kelly's
Ford

15

29   Tinpot Run

Remington

AP

Hubbard   Run

15 29

Rappahannock

I-III *Rock Garden*

Marsh Run

N

Kelly's Ford   I-III *Rock Garden*

W   E

S

River

0   1   2

Miles

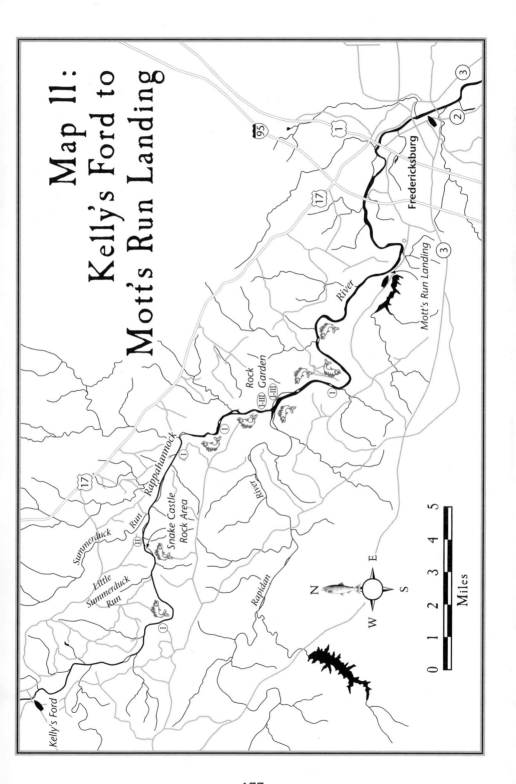

Map 11:
Kelly's Ford to
Mott's Run Landing

Fredericksburg

Mott's Run Landing

River

Rock Garden

Rappahannock

River

Summerduck Run

Snake Castle Rock Area

Little Summerduck Run

Rapidan

Kelly's Ford

Miles

N W E S

0 1 2 3 4 5

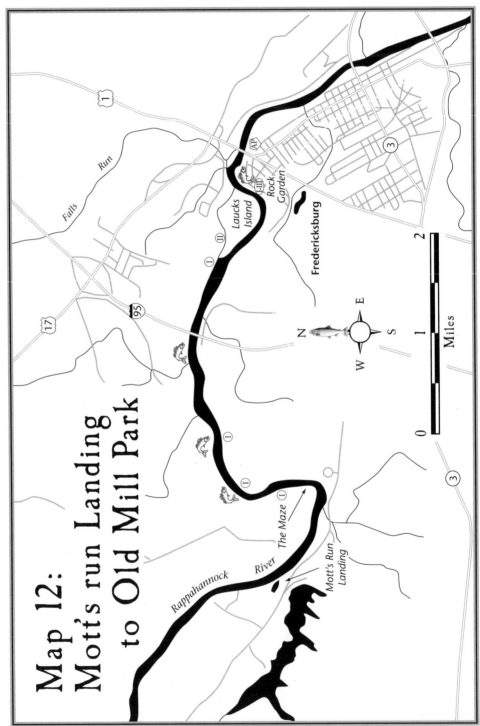

Map 12:
Mott's run Landing
to Old Mill Park

INDEX